PERSONALITY THEORIES
Journeys Into Self

AN EXPERIENTIAL WORKBOOK

SECOND EDITION

Willard B. Frick

Teachers College, Columbia University
New York and London

Published by Teachers College Press, 1234 Amsterdam Avenue
New York, NY 10027

Photo credits: p. 8 – Sigmund Freud (Courtesy of the Austrian Press and Information Service, New York); p. 21 – Alfred Adler (Courtesy of the Alfred Adler Institute, Chicago); p. 38 – Carl Jung (Courtesy of the Bettmann Archive); p. 49 – Karen Horney (Courtesy of the Association for the Advancement of Psychoanalysis, Inc. of the Karen Horney Psychoanalytic Institute and Center); p. 62 – Erik Erikson (Courtesy of Harvard University News Office); p. 73 – Albert Bandura (Courtesy of Albert Bandura); p. 85 – Gordon Allport (Courtesy of Harvard University News Office); p. 96 – Abraham Maslow (Courtesy of Brandeis University Public Affairs Office); p. 108 – Carl Rogers (Courtesy of the Center for Studies of the Person)

Printed on acid-free paper

Manufactured in the United States of America

98 97 96 95 94 93 92 91 8 7 6 5 4 3 2 1

For Tom, Ian, and Cristina

Contents

Preface to the Second Edition

The second edition of a book means, among other things, that the first effort, while not without flaws, has been a success. It is very gratifying, therefore, to present this second edition of *Personality Theories: Journeys Into Self* to you and to know that this experiential workbook has been of value to many teachers and their students. Those of you who have used the first edition will recognize that the present one has been strengthened in many ways.

It is enormously satisfying for me to know—to have confirmed—that self-learning can be successfully integrated with theoretical learning to enhance the meaning and significance of both. After my experience with this book, I am even more convinced that psychological theories divorced from one's experiences are dry bones, without flesh and substance.

Publishing a book is a team effort, and two of the most important members of this team have been Brian Ellerbeck and Cathy McClure of Teachers College Press. They have supported and directed this revision project with much patience, superb editorial skills, and sincere personal interest. I wish to thank them both for maintaining such high standards throughout the process.

For the preparation of the manuscript for this second edition I am indebted to Erika Flores of the Psychology Department at Albion College. Her expertise, cooperation, and sustaining good humor are greatly appreciated.

Willard B. Frick
Albion College
June 1990

Acknowledgments

The development of this book was initiated with a grant from the Mellon Foundation, which was administered by Albion College. I would like to express my appreciation for their support.

I wish to thank my friend and colleague Berne Jacobs of Kalamazoo College for his generosity in reading portions of the manuscript and providing me with many helpful suggestions.

I wish to thank also Patricia Frick, Albion College, for her strong support and sustained interest in this project. She was also a helpful consultant during the development of the book.

Finally, I wish to thank Dr. Albert Bandura for his review of my unit on social learning theory and Dr. Heinz Ansbacher for his review of the unit on Alfred Adler. They both provided me with some very helpful comments and suggestions.

The workbook in its entirety stands, of course, as my own responsibility.

Notes to the Student

This experiential workbook in personality theory is for you. While I believe it will make the teaching of personality theory more exciting for your instructor, the book is primarily for you, the student. It includes material that will help you relate the abstract theories and concepts of personality theory to your own personality development and life experience. This will enable you to give these concepts an important reality within the context of your development and experiences and to activate many of them as constructive forces in your own life.

Although I have provided an informative introduction to each exercise, these introductions are in no way a substitute for your textbook material. *It is essential* that you understand the theoretical and conceptual material of each theorist *before* you approach the related exercises.

In this book you will be asked to reflect upon many aspects of your experience and to examine your experiences from different perspectives. Each of the nine personality theorists included makes different assumptions about the nature of human personality and its development. Some of their perspectives will be more compatible with your own assumptions and personal experience than others. But perhaps you will also discover that each theorist has something to say to you and that each in his or her own way supplies at least one important piece to the complex mosaic of human personality.

In order to receive maximum value from the workbook, you will need to give thoughtful attention to each exercise. I suggest that each day you set aside some quiet time for reflection on the exercises you are working on. In this way, your work can become an experience in guided meditation.

Above all, I hope your work on these exercises will be enjoyable. Most of the students in my classes who have had an opportunity to use this book have enjoyed the experience of getting to know themselves better in this way. Many students keep the workbook as an important personal record. You may want to do this and refer to it again at a later time.

Notes to the Instructor

If there is any single course in the psychology curriculum that should provide students with opportunities to relate concepts and theories to their own lives, it is a course in personality theory. It was my frustration in trying to provide such experiences for my students that led me to develop this book. The use of this material has enriched my teaching and has made my course in personality theory much more interesting and valuable to my students.

This workbook has been designed to supplement most introductory textbooks in personality theory. The nine theorists included here are basic to the study of personality and have been selected because of the relevance of their theories to human experience and the ease with which those theories can be applied to the lives of students.

Some of these exercises ask for responses that draw upon intimate personal experience. In my use of the workbook, however, I have never had a student who was upset by this or who felt that such exercises were an invasion of his or her privacy. Most students appreciate this opportunity to explore important aspects of their private experience in this focused and disciplined way.

Most of the exercises can be done by the student as assignments outside the classroom. These are the exercises that ask the students to write on their most intimate experiences and are not to be shared in the classroom. I have, however, included several classroom exercises that do call for small-group discussion or the interaction of students in pairs. These classroom exercises have enlivened and enriched my own classes in personality theory, and I recommend them to you. They are relevant to text material and at the same time draw upon those personal experiences that most students are enthusiastic about sharing and discussing with their peers.

I have found that these discussion exercises are much more active and open in small groups than when the entire class is involved. My own teaching situation, with 25 to 35 students, allows me to form small discussion groups within the classroom. I also make use of nearby classrooms, when available, for these activities. Many classes will have considerably more students. If that is your situation, with some flexibility and creativity, you can arrange to adapt these in-class exercises to fit your own teaching situation. I can almost guarantee that these in-class discussion exercises will be rewarding for both you and your students.

My own way of using this workbook is to have students turn in a completed unit every week, since this time schedule roughly corresponds to their text reading and to the lectures. You may need a different schedule. I alone read each unit that the students complete, assuring them of confidentiality, and make written comments in the workbook when I feel they are appropriate and helpful. I give each completed unit a plus or minus evaluation. Most minus grades result from a lack of time and thoughtful attention given to the exercises. The few students who receive a minus have the option of rewriting the unit. You will, of course, have your own way of working with this material and may prefer not to evaluate it at all.

Whatever your approach, I believe that your use of this book will not only enhance student learning but will also make your teaching more exciting and enjoyable.

Childhood Recollections and Experiences

A. **Family Photographs**
B. **Drawing Your House Plan**
C. **Sharing Memories: The Guided Tour**
D. **Family Mealtime: Togetherness and Conflict**
E. **Summary Exercise**

The past does not place an indelible stamp on your personality, but it does become an important part of who you are. As you will discover, most personality theorists emphasize the importance of past experience in the development of personality, although their views differ on just how these early experiences influence development.

Throughout this book you will be drawing upon your own experiences, past and present. The four introductory exercises that follow are not related to any specific theory of personality development but are designed to increase your awareness and stimulate your self-reflections.

The following exercises will stimulate your memory of events, scenes, and emotional experiences of your childhood. They will help you explore some roots of your present development. By reconstructing the physical and emotional settings in which your early development took place, perhaps you will discover something meaningful.

A. FAMILY PHOTOGRAPHS

For most families, family photographs form an essential and cherished documentary of its life and times. Collectively, these family photographs richly portray a shared history of experiences and the growth and development of individual members of the family.

Occasionally, prompted by some inner searching, we seek out these photographs, finding them in dusty albums or tucked away, almost forgotten, in the nooks and crannies of our homes. In these encounters with the past, we renew our sense of mystery and fascination with our family experience.

A thoughtful study of family photographs can provide us with helpful insights into family dynamics and relationships and into our own development within the family structure. The following exercise will help you explore these possibilities by examining a selection of your own family photographs.

Collect 10 to 15 family photographs that represent a span of years in your development. As you study each one, please give your attention to the following possibilities.

- Is someone's "body language" evident in the photographs? That is, is there any significant position or way of holding the body that reflects a certain attitude or role within the family?
- Is emotional closeness and/or emotional distance suggested by some features in the photographs?
- Is there an "insider" or an "outsider" in the family system that is evident in the photographs? Is there a family member who is never in the picture? Does one of your family members suggest detachment, always off to one side? Is someone always in the center of the pictures?
- Are you or one of your siblings usually in a favored position, standing or sitting between your parents?
- Is there a relationship between individual positions in the photographs and the usual relationships and interaction within the family?

Please be cautious about overinterpreting a *single* photograph. The more pictures you have of you and your family the greater the likelihood of discovering a pattern or central themes.

Exercise 1

Do your photographs tell a story about you and your family? Discuss your major observations, discoveries, and feelings that have emerged from a thoughtful examination of your family photographs.

B. DRAWING YOUR HOUSE PLAN

Exercise 2

a. On the next page, draw a floor plan of the house you lived in that was most important to you before you were 10 years old. After you complete the drawing, sit quietly and try to recapture the sights and sounds and smells of each room and the experiences and feelings you associate with each.

b. Who lived in this house with you?

c. What was your favorite place? Why?

d. Where were your secret places? What did you do there that was important to you?

FLOOR PLAN OF MY HOUSE

e. What room or area of the house do you remember as the most unpleasant or uncomfortable for you? Why?

f. What was the prevailing atmosphere or mood in your house?

g. What was your most significant experience during the time you lived in this house? How was this experience significant? In other words, what did you learn from it? What impact did it have on your development?

C. SHARING MEMORIES: THE GUIDED TOUR

Classroom Exercise

After you have drawn the plan of your house and explored it in privacy, select a partner in the class and take him or her on a "tour" of your house, sharing as many of your feelings and associations as you feel comfortable with. Describe your house in such a way that your partner gets a "feel" for what your experience in your house was like. When you have finished, your partner will take you on a tour of his or her house. (If it is not feasible to do this exercise in class, make arrangements to do it outside class.)

D. FAMILY MEALTIME: TOGETHERNESS AND CONFLICT

Most families come together at mealtime. It is a time for shared experience, conversation, and family interaction. The dining table frequently becomes, therefore, the center for both togetherness and conflict, and the dynamics of family relationships are often revealed in the interactions that take place there.

Exercise 3

Think about your early experiences with your family at mealtime. What mood prevailed? Try to get in touch with your feelings and perceptions during these family interactions. Try to recall specific scenes and conversations. Describe these feelings and perceptions and briefly discuss the personal impact of these mealtime experiences.

E. SUMMARY EXERCISE

What are some important things you have learned about yourself after doing these introductory exercises? Which was the most valuable exercise for you? Why?

Classroom Exercise

Join a small discussion group and share with one another what you learned and found important in this unit. After 20 minutes come together as a whole class and discuss your major learnings.

Sigmund Freud and Psychoanalytic Theory

A. **Dreamwork**
B. **Anxiety**
C. **Ego-Defense Mechanisms**
D. **Free Association and Resistance**
E. **Transference**
F. **Summary Exercise**

Freud has the distinction of being the first, and most nearly comprehensive, personality theorist. With the exception of Bandura and, perhaps, Rogers, he helped lay the foundation for all of the other theories presented in this book, theories that either built upon his ideas or developed as a reaction against them.

While dramatic revisions of Freudian theory have taken place in recent years, it continues to have a profound influence on our Western culture. Freud's ideas are the mainstay of critical analysis in art, music, literature, and biographical study.

Freud, one of the premier minds in the history of Western thought, was certainly aware of his own importance. He compared his shattering influence on our self–world view to that of Copernicus, who taught us that the earth was not the center of our solar system, and to that of Darwin, who rejected the premise of "special creation." Freud's special blow to our self-esteem lay in his clinical evidence that we are irrational creatures, driven by instincts and controlled by unconscious motivations.

According to Hjelle and Ziegler (1981) the three strongest, most basic assumptions of Freudian theory are

1. *Its deterministic view of personality development.* In Freudian theory there is little room for freedom of choice and self-determination. Behavior is largely determined by instinctual drives and unconscious forces.
2. *Its belief in the irrationality of the human personality.* With the exception of a small sphere of rationality within the ego that may be enlarged and strengthened through psychoanalysis, the personality is hostage to irrational forces.
3. *Its view of the unchanging nature of personality.* The personality is shaped and determined in infancy and early childhood. This basic personality structure remains unchanged throughout the adult years. There are only variations on the old theme of instinct control with the hope of achieving some positive expressions and productive work through sublimation. Even in psychoanalysis, however, no fundamental changes are considered possible.

All personality theories have some measure of validity in helping us understand significant aspects of our development. In the following exercises, perhaps you can get in touch with some experiences that help validate certain aspects of Freudian theory.

A. DREAMWORK

Dreams have a very important place in Freudian theory and analysis. Dreams were, for Freud, the "royal road" to the unconscious. They were symbols, distorted substitutes for unconscious thoughts, feelings, and desires. Because of this distortion, the dream was seen in two aspects: (1) the *manifest content* — the remembered and conscious part of the dream — the dream as we usually tell it to another person; (2) the *latent content* — the most important dimension of the dream for Freud, which includes aspects of the dream that are symbolized and distorted. Such distortions reflect or contain deeper meanings that are often out of the reach of awareness of the dreamer.

According to Freud's theory, the true purpose of the dream is to fulfill wishes and impulses in an imaginary fashion. These are presented in the dream in symbolic disguise in order to protect the individual from anxiety and psychic pain.

Exercise 1

Keep this workbook by your bed and record your dreams for a full week. If you are awakened by a dream, turn on your light (a pen light is helpful here) and write down the dream immediately. Don't lose it. Capture the essence of your dream at the moment or you will be likely to forget it.

First, write down the manifest content of your dreams, then select one dream for discussion of its latent content. See if you can probe into some possible meanings and significance of this dream. Take some time for reflection, writing down all associations that you have with each aspect of the dream. Can you relate some of these associations to your present anxieties, wishes, and fears?

WEEK'S RECORD OF DREAMS
MANIFEST CONTENT

Dream # 1 — Manifest Content

Dream # 2 — Manifest Content

Dream # 3 — Manifest Content

LATENT CONTENT FOR DREAM # _____

B. ANXIETY

One important caveat should be presented here before you tackle the experience of anxiety and continue on in the workbook. The experience of anxiety is a normal experience, even a constructive one for most of us most of the time. It may frequently serve to increase alertness and enhance performance. It is not, however, unusual for us to experience excessive anxiety, at times, that might be explained by the Freudian model. In any case, to suffer from anxiety occasionally does not make us neurotic. This principle holds true for other theories in this workbook that deal with the problem of anxiety and other neurotic developments in the personality.

Anxiety can, however, be one of the most distressing emotional states we can experience. It is characterized by vague feelings of apprehension, premonitions of danger, and disquieting feelings of impending crisis. Because of its painful nature, we are driven, through healthy or unhealthy strategies, to prevent its occurrence or reduce its intensity. Anxiety is an inevitable aspect of our lives, an aspect of being-in-the-world, and managing this emotion successfully is a key to healthy development. It is not surprising, therefore, that the concept of anxiety plays a central role in personality theory.

While there are differences of opinion about the object of anxiety or its basic source, most personality theorists would agree that anxiety represents the perception of some fundamental threat to our existence.

Anxiety plays a prominent role in Freud's theory of personality development. Although his interpretation of anxiety went through several stages of development, as did many aspects of his theory, in its final stage Freud saw anxiety as an ego function, and he emphasized the important signal function of anxiety in alerting the ego to impending danger.

Freud viewed the ego as responding to threat or potential danger from three primary sources: the environment, id impulses, and the superego. Freud thus identified three primary types of anxiety.

1. *Reality Anxiety* reflects the ego's dependence on the external world, where the environment represents an objective source of danger. This type of anxiety comes the closest to representing an objective, tangible fear state (e.g., anxiety over possible loss of a scholarship) and is least likely to become neurotic in intensity.
2. *Neurotic Anxiety* reflects the ego's dependence on the id and arises when the ego feels pressure from primitive impulses that threaten to become conscious and push the person to behave in an impulsive or destructive manner. Neurotic anxiety is the ego's alarm system, a signal that id impulses are pressing for release and expression. In its original manifestation, neurotic anxiety is identified by its vagueness and ambiguity. Thus, the vague apprehension, dread, and discomfort one feels in neurotic anxiety (without a tangible object as in reality anxiety) is one of its central features. The unconscious dimension of mental life is obviously at work here. As a means of coping with such anxiety, however, these nebulous feelings may become attached to an object or concrete situation. Neurotic anxiety in this case can often be identified by intensity of emotion and exaggerated behavior, as in a phobia or panic when one is in an elevator.
3. *Moral Anxiety* suggests the ego's dependence upon the superego and is aroused when there is a conflict between the ego and superego, for example, when the id strives toward some immoral thought or action. The superego, as the moral arm

and conscience of the psyche, may also become a threat to the ego's expression of normal developmental needs. Doing or thinking something contrary to the super-ego (internalized parental standards) may provoke fears of punishment and arouse intense anxiety and feelings of guilt.

Exercise 2

With these three basic types of anxiety in mind, reflect upon your own experiences with "being anxious" and see if you can identify each type as an occasional source of anxiety in your own life.

For each type of anxiety, describe the situation in which you became anxious and the feelings and consequences of the anxiety.

- An experience I have had that illustrates reality anxiety.

- An experience I have had that illustrates neurotic anxiety.

- An experience I have had that illustrates moral anxiety.

C. EGO-DEFENSE MECHANISMS

We all use psychic defensive strategies to protect ourselves from the threat of anxiety. For Freud the concept of *psychic defense* was a major psychodynamic principle and referred to a protective process designed to shield the ego from painful and unacceptable thoughts and anxiety-arousing impulses.

Exercise 3

a. Try to become aware of the role that each mechanism plays in your defense system. Under each defense mechanism write down how important you feel it is as a current ego defense in your life. Place an asterisk (*) next to those of greatest service to you. Try to present specific examples of how each operates in your life. Before responding to this exercise, be sure that the definition of each of the following five defense mechanisms is clear in your mind.

Projection

Rationalization

Denial

Regression

Sublimation

b. We are vulnerable creatures, and defense mechanisms may serve a very valuable purpose in our lives. They can, however, become disruptive and self-defeating. In general, defense mechanisms distort reality and may seduce us into inaccurate perceptions and inappropriate behavior. Thus, if certain defenses become habitual and dominant in our lives, they may inhibit personal growth. (Freud considered sublimation to be the only healthy and positive mechanism of defense.) Do you feel that your use of a given defense mechanism is destructive to you or has interfered with your life in any important ways? Discuss.

D. FREE ASSOCIATION AND RESISTANCE

Free association is a psychoanalytic technique to uncover repression and to bring the unconscious into consciousness. One of the difficulties that Freud and other practitioners experienced with the technique was the phenomenon of *resistance* that the patient often maintained to protect the ego. You will experience both the technique and the problem of resistance in the following exercise.

Exercise 4

a. In an atmosphere of quiet privacy, tape record your free associations for a 15-minute period. Try to suspend all concern about meaning, logical connections, or social convention. Allow yourself to verbalize any words, thoughts, or feelings that come to you during the period. Remember, do not try to control your thoughts or censor or analyze them. Just let them come as they will.

Immediately following your 15-minute period of free association, record your experience in doing this exercise. How did you feel? What were your major forms of resistance in carrying out this exercise? Discuss.

Perhaps you have gained some insight into the difficulties this technique presents for both the patient and the therapist.

b. After several days, play back your free associations. What are your reactions now on listening to this material? Do you have any new associations or meanings?

E. TRANSFERENCE

Transference is a phenomenon frequently encountered by both analyst and patient during psychoanalysis. It is a type of displacement in which the patient (and/or analyst) expresses and acts out both verbally and nonverbally certain impulses, wishes, and feelings that were initially held toward another individual early in the life of the patient. For example, repressed anger and resentment (and/or love) toward one's mother or father may be expressed during the transference as hostility and anger toward the analyst. Such feelings, when displaced in the transference, are usually excessive and are expressed in inappropriate ways.

It is not necessary to undergo an analysis, however, to experience the working of this phenomenon in our own lives. Frequently we encounter an individual upon whom we displace or "transfer" needs and feelings that have been with us from childhood. These individuals take on a special meaning in our lives and are the object of our projected or transferred needs and feelings. This transference phenomenon will often reveal itself, for example, when we become aware of unusually strong feelings toward a person whom we do not really know very well. The feelings, objectively speaking, are *inappropriate* since they are *not* based on adequate knowledge of or experience with the other person.

Exercise 5

Think of a faculty member, employer, or other adult (avoid those your own age) toward whom you have had strong and unexplained feelings. These feelings may be extremely positive (special attraction) or negative (anxiety, extreme dislike) or may include elements of both.

a. First, tell the objective facts about your relationship with this person, such as length and nature of the relationship.

b. Describe your strong feelings and reactions toward this person that might indicate that some element of transference is a determining factor in your response to him or her.

c. Consider the possibility that your response may be a type of transference and that you may actually be expressing certain repressed and unresolved needs and feelings in relation to your parents. Allow yourself some time to consider this and then write down the *emotional connections* you may have established between your relationship with one of your parents and the transference figure. Specifically, what needs and impulses have you displaced onto the transference figure?

d. After bringing these displaced feelings into greater awareness, do you think you can feel differently about the transference figure? Can the relationship become a different one? (You may want to return to this question after a period of time.)

F. SUMMARY EXERCISE

What are some of the important things you have learned about yourself after doing these exercises on Freudian theory? Which was the most valuable exercise for you? Why?

Classroom Exercise

Join a small discussion group and share with one another what you learned and found important in this unit. After 20 to 30 minutes come together as a whole class and discuss your major learnings.

Alfred Adler
and
Individual Psychology

A. Early Recollections
B. Inferiority Feelings
C. Birth Order and Personality
   Development
D. Fictional Final Goal
E. Style of Life
F. Social Interest
G. Summary Exercise

In 1902, after publishing a paper defending Freud's book, *The Interpretation of Dreams*, Adler was invited by Freud to join the elite Vienna Psychoanalytic Society. Thus, as a member of this inner circle, he became one of Freud's earliest associates. But Adler's growing dissatisfaction with Freud's view of infantile sexuality and his emphasis on the unconscious mind seriously compromised his standing with Freud and the Society. Thus, in 1911, only a year after he had served as president, Adler resigned from this prestigious group.

Soon after his resignation, Adler and his followers formed their own group known, initially, as the Society of Free Psychoanalytic Research. Later, the group adopted "individual psychology" to more clearly identify their commitment to a different set of assumptions about human personality.

Adler not only proved to be a gifted personality theorist but also became a pioneer in the field of community psychiatry. A leader in the development of child guidance clinics, he applied his personality theories in a helpful and practical way to the areas of child development, education, psychotherapy, and family counseling. Gradually, these important theoretical and practical contributions brought Adler wide recognition, and he was in demand as a lecturer all over the world. It was while he was on one of his many lecture tours that he died of a heart attack in May 1937.

Following his death Adler's impact waned. For the past two decades, however, owing in no small measure to the interpretive work of Heinz and Rowena Ansbacher, Adler's theories have once again become well known and influential.

There is a journal devoted to the theory and practice of individual psychology, and many active centers for Adlerian study exist throughout the world. Several of these centers, including the Alfred Adler Institute in Chicago, offer advanced degrees in the theory and practice of individual psychology.

Over the years, Adler has also been extremely influential on other psychologists and the development of their ideas. These include, among many others, Abraham Maslow, Carl Rogers, Gordon Allport, Rollo May, Karen Horney, and Eric Fromm.

Adler's theories and their applications continue to be substantive and relevant to our life and times.

A. EARLY RECOLLECTIONS

To understand a man we must know his memories. — Ancient Chinese Proverb

Early recollections were also extremely significant to Alfred Adler as a way of understanding the personality and current life-style of the individual; he considered the discovery of the significance of early memories to be one of the most important findings of individual psychology. According to Adler there are no random selections or "chance memories." Of the thousands upon thousands of possibilities, you will remember those events and experiences that express and reinforce the most important aspects of your *present* personality; your philosophy of life, your anxieties; your ambitions and goals, and so forth. In capsule, your earliest recollections will reveal important aspects of your current *style of life*. One's earliest memories will, therefore, have purpose and meaning.

It is not important whether your earliest recollections are entirely accurate or not. It is the *way* you remember certain experiences in your life that is the most important thing. It is your consistent life-style *now* that determines what and how you remember.

In doing the following exercise it is important to distinguish between recollections and reports. A recollection is a specific memory (e.g., on my first day of school an older boy pushed me down. I cried and ran to find the teacher), whereas a report is only a general memory (e.g., I remember that we always went to my grandparents' house on Christmas day). For the purpose of this exercise, you are to present early recollections and not general reports.

Exercise 1

Beginning with your first recollection, identify five of your earliest specific memories. Present as many details as possible, including important feelings and emotions.

Memory #1

Memory #2

Memory #3

Memory #4

Memory #5

PRINCIPLES OF INTERPRETATION AND SUGGESTIONS
FOR WORKING WITH EARLY RECOLLECTIONS

- If your recollections seem inconsistent, look for a pattern and unifying themes.
- Trivial events may be more significant than spectacular ones.
- In your recollections, is the environment friendly or hostile? Recounting accidents, dangers, and punishments may reflect a perception of the world as dangerous.
- Recalling the birth of a sibling may suggest feelings of dethronement.
- Are you usually alone or with others?
- Are you cooperative or competitive in your recollections?
- Are you active or passive in your early memories? For example, passive individuals often report watching events or other people.
- Is one of your recollections centered on your first day at school? This recollection usually indicates an attitude toward new situations.

These are just some suggestions for interpretation. Remember that you will want to look for recurring themes and unifying connections in your recollections.

Exercise 2

Reflect upon your early memories and the meaning they have for you now. What seem to be the unifying themes? Do your earliest recollections suggest anything to you about your present personality? In your discussion, identify each memory by its number.

B. INFERIORITY FEELINGS

In Adler's early work, *inferiority feelings* formed the basis for all human motivation and striving. Adler related these feelings to a sense of incompletion, insecurity,
and being in a minus situation. His original theory grew in large part from his own
experience with physical weakness and from his belief that sickness and disability
produced a sense of inferiority. This became the primary factor leading to strivings
for superiority and to the development of the strengths and skills of personality.

Later, Adler expanded his theory of inferiority in two important respects. First,
he emphasized that inferiority feelings can come from *perceived* psychological or
social handicaps, as well as from physically based disabilities. Second, Adler placed
more and more emphasis on the *striving for superiority* as a primary motivation and
not merely a compensation for inferiority feelings. Thus, the equation might look
like this:

Inferiority feelings + striving for superiority = goal direction and life style.

Adler cited three conditions of early childhood that could lead to a complex of inferiority feelings: (1) organ inferiority, (2) excessive indulgence and pampering, (3) and
rejection and neglect.

Exercise 3

a. What do you regard as the major source of your feelings of inferiority as a
child? Try to remember *specific* incidents and experiences that contributed to or
reinforced these feelings. Can you relate these feelings of inferiority to one of Adler's
three conditions, or have you identified a different condition for your feelings?

b. Were your early experiences with inferiority feelings suggested in your earliest memories? Reread your early recollections before responding.

c. What specific connections can you make between your awareness of childhood feelings of inferiority and later strivings for excellence and superiority? Discuss.

d. According to Adler, the inferiority–superiority dynamic remains an important force throughout our lives. How is this dynamic reflected in your life at the present time? Is there an area of felt inadequacy and inferiority that you are currently striving to overcome?

C. BIRTH ORDER AND PERSONALITY DEVELOPMENT

An important subjective influence on personality development, according to Adler, is the order of birth within the family constellation. Owing to the order of birth, the psychological situation in the home will be different for each child. Thus, although born of the same parents and growing up in the same home, each successive child will develop within a different environment and will approach his or her situation from a unique perspective. Birth order becomes an important variable in generating inferiority feelings, as well as strategies for achieving superiority.

The Oldest Child. The firstborn child eventually faces the crisis of "dethronement." With the new arrival he or she is likely to feel displaced, with a loss of power and control. As a compensation, the oldest child may later enjoy exercises of authority, tend toward conservatism, and exaggerate the importance of authority, rules, and laws. Adler observed that a greater proportion of problem children are oldest children.

If the firstborn feels loved, however, and is adequately prepared for the new arrival, the negative influences of dethronement may be minimized.

The Second Child. The second child must share attention from the very beginning of life. One of the primary motivations of the second born is to catch up with and surpass the older sibling. The second child often behaves, therefore, as if in a race and, in an effort to compete successfully with the older sibling, may set his or her goals too high. The second child, Adler observed, is often more talented and successful than the firstborn.

The Youngest Child. The youngest child has the advantage of having pacemakers within the family and is highly motivated to excel older brothers and sisters. The ultimate success of the youngest child in surpassing siblings has been a major theme in many myths and fairy tales from a variety of different cultures. Because of a desire to excel in everything, however, the youngest child may fail to develop one central ambition. Also, the youngest child is usually pampered and has difficulty achieving independence. This situation may lead to feelings of inferiority.

The Only Child. Having no siblings, the only child directs his or her feelings toward the mother and father.

The only child is usually pampered by the mother and needs to be the center of attention at all times. For this reason the only child may become self-centered and fail to develop socially.

Adler also observed that the only child may reflect a timid or anxious environment created by parents who fear or do not want additional children.

It is quite apparent that each birth order contains both advantages and disadvantages for the development of the personality. We must recognize, also, that there are many other variables at work within a given family constellation. Such factors as age difference between children and the sex of each child will also be important influences in shaping the child's environment.

Exercise 4

Do your experiences within your family confirm or contradict Adler's observations on the impact of birth order on personality? Describe your situation, evaluate, and discuss.

Classroom Exercise

Form small discussion groups of students of the same birth order — the oldest child, the middle child, the youngest, and the only child — and discuss the ways in which you feel your unique position in the family influenced you and how you influenced your family. Examine both positive and negative influences. After 20 to 30 minutes of small-group interaction, come together as a class to share experiences and conclusions. (If small groups are not feasible for this exercise, find a partner of the same birth order outside class.)

D. FICTIONAL FINAL GOAL

Many students find Adler's concept of the *fictional final goal* confusing. Some brief comments may help clarify it.

Adler believed that our primary goal in life is subjectively determined, created by us, and largely unconscious. Hence his use of the term *fictional*. According to Adler, the deepest, most pervasive goal in one's life has little or no objective basis in reality but is based on privately held beliefs and values. In important ways, of course, our fictional final goal is closely related to our sovereign striving for perfection and overcoming of inferiority. This goal is uniquely our own and is formed out of the fundamental needs and experiences of childhood. The fictional goal was, for Adler, the goal around which all psychic life is integrated, forming a unified pattern of upward movement throughout one's life.

In doing these exercises, remember to distinguish between your fictional goal and your more concrete goals. Your concrete goals serve the purpose of advancing you toward the realization of your fictional final goal. The following exercises ask you to identify and become more aware of this fictional final goal in your life.

Exercise 5

a. The incomplete sentences that follow are designed to aid you in becoming more aware of your fictional final goal. Although Adler believed this goal to be largely unconscious, it is possible to become more aware of it and how it functions in your life.

Complete the following sentences. Do not ponder each one but write down your initial and spontaneous response.

1. I usually feel that my future will . . .

2. I look forward to the time when . . .

3. I always seem to be striving for . . .

4. One of the most important things that keeps me going is my belief that . . .

5. My fundamental vision of my future is . . .

6. I am most highly motivated by the value I place on . . .

   b. Consider your responses to the incomplete sentences above. Do they seem to reveal something of your fictional final goal in life? Discuss.

   c. State what you feel is the most basic and pervasive fictional final goal in your life and indicate, with examples, how this goal guides your actions and motives. Which sentence-completion item most clearly reflects this goal?

E. STYLE OF LIFE

Style of life was a primary theme in Adler's later writings. Adler had a very specific meaning for his concept of *life-style*, which is different from the popular use of the term today. In Adlerian theory, style of life refers to the basic approach to life that enhances the goal of superiority. Our style of life is composed of those unique characteristics that identify the personality, including basic attitudes toward the self, our worldview, and our pattern of traits, behaviors, and values. We all have developed unique and patterned ways of responding to our early feelings of inferiority in an effort to defend ourselves against such feelings and achieve superiority and perfection. This is our style of life.

Rudiments of our life-style develop early, according to Adler, so that by the time we are 4 or 5 years old these patterns are already well established as a basic and relatively permanent structure. The childhood beginnings of life-style emerge out of one's early experience and become a relatively enduring feature of personality. For this reason, as we have seen, Adler felt that one's *earliest memories* and perception of these remembered events are good vehicles for gaining an insight into important aspects of our current life-style.

You may wish to reread your record of early recollections and the work done for this exercise as one means of gaining insight into your basic style of life (basic attitudes, approaches to life, perceptions of the world, and so forth).

Exercise 6

a. Adler (1969) observed that "As long as a person is in a favorable situation we cannot see his life-style clearly. In new situations, however, where he is confronted with difficulties, the style of life appears clearly and distinctly" (p. 38).

In addition to early recollections, therefore, another means suggested by Adler of gaining insight into your life-style is to appraise your responses to a life crisis or an extremely difficult situation. Think of a new and difficult situation you have experienced in your life and how you responded to it. Did your response or method of coping with the experience reveal basic attitudes, perceptions of the self, and an approach to life that suggest your basic style of life? Identify your situation, your way of dealing with it, and its significance in revealing important aspects of your life-style.

b. Adler, like Freud, believed that these basic life-style patterns and structures of personality are established relatively early in life — by the time the child goes to school. Do you find that this has been true for you? Are there important features or characteristics of your present personality that were taking shape and exhibited in childhood? If so, these may represent enduring features of your life-style.

Discuss important childhood characteristics and trends that continue to be manifest in your personality. Be specific and provide examples, if possible.

Exercise 7

Adler identified four basic types of people according to their life-style attitudes:

1. *The ruling type.* These are assertive, aggressive individuals who tend to dominate others and have a low degree of social awareness and interest.
2. *The getting type.* These individuals tend to lean on others and to take much more than they give.
3. *The avoiding type.* These individuals tend to avoid the problems of life, and they participate very little in socially useful activity.
4. *The socially useful type.* These individuals have a high degree of social interest and activity.

Consider all of your observations and statements on your life-style made in the exercises above. Which one (or two) of Adler's life-style attitudes do you feel you most closely represent? Discuss.

F. SOCIAL INTEREST

In his later writings, Adler placed more and more emphasis on *social interest* as the highest expression of the mature personality. Social feeling, community interest, and helping to bring about an ideal community are important aspects of Adler's concept of social interest.

Exercise 8

    a. To what degree does your life reflect this measure of personal maturity and psychological health? Discuss.

    b. List specific ways in which you have contributed to or are now contributing to the welfare of others, to the community, and to raising the quality of life for the well-being of others.

c. Do you feel that you have neglected this area of your personality development? If so, can you attribute this to your early experience in the family? (Adler believed that social interest was fostered or inhibited in the home.) Discuss.

d. What present opportunities do you have to explore and deepen your social interest? Make a list of currently available organizations and projects that offer you the opportunity for community or social service. Which opportunity to express your social interest appeals to you the most? Why?

G. SUMMARY EXERCISE

What are some of the important things you have learned about yourself after doing these exercises on Adler's theory of personality? Which was the most valuable exercise for you. Why?

Classroom Exercise

Join a small discussion group and share with one another what you learned and found important in this unit. After 20 minutes come together as a whole class and discuss your major learnings.

Carl Jung
and
Analytical Psychology

A. The Collective Unconscious—
   The Archetypes
B. The Structure of Consciousness—
   The Basic Attitudes of Extraversion
   and Introversion
C. The Four Functions of Consciousness—
   Thinking, Feeling, Sensing, and
   Intuiting
D. Summary Exercise

Carl Jung stands as a monumental figure in the history of psychology. Although his influence has not been as pervasive as Freud's, his unique theoretical contributions to our understanding of personality have been considerable.

Jung was, perhaps, the most scholarly of all the personality theorists, and though his theories were derived primarily from his experiences with patients in psychotherapy, he also drew upon important secondary sources in support of his ideas. In addition to his own medical and psychiatric training, Jung had a scholarly command of comparative religion, mythology, cultural anthropology, philosophy, and history. In important ways, Jung brought his vast storehouse of knowledge from many disciplines to bear on his multidimensional theory, a theory that recognized the wholeness, uniqueness, and the deep creative resources of the human personality.

A. THE COLLECTIVE UNCONSCIOUS—THE ARCHETYPES

Jung's greatest contribution to our understanding of personality was his theory of the collective unconscious and its archetypes. With this theory Jung added a significant new dimension to our concept of the unconscious, which, until his theory, had been limited to the repression of *individual* feelings and experiences. This view of the unconscious as an individual phenomenon was the one developed by Freud. In sharp contrast, the collective unconscious recognized the primordial imprinting of important species experiences that have been shared throughout human history. We have, in other words, inherited the potential for thought and response patterns, symbols, and images that have emerged from the most central experiences of the human race. Thus, for Jung, the collective unconscious represents a creative resource rather than a defensive system.

These primordial images or collective symbols Jung called *archetypes*. Each archetype represents a certain psychic disposition and potential. From the dawn of human consciousness, for example, the human race has shared the experiences of mothers, birth, death, God, power, magic, the hero, the stranger, and prejudice. Each of these psychic motifs in our lives can be traced back to earliest human history.

As Jung (cited in Campbell, 1971) emphasized, "There are as many archetypes as there are typical situations in life. Endless repetition has engraved these experiences into one's psychic constitution, not in the form of images filled with content, but at first only as *forms without content*, representing merely the possibility of a certain type of perception and action" (p. 66).

Let us begin our exercises by drawing upon Jung's supreme theoretical achievement, the collective unconscious and its archetypes. Although much of this archetypical material remains unindividuated, lying within the collective darkness of the unconscious, many aspects are available for individuation. Perhaps we can make some conscious contact with a few of the important archetypes.

The Persona.   The persona is the side of the personality that one presents publicly. It exhibits those aspects of personality that are acceptable to others. To put our "best foot forward" reduces conflict by meeting the needs and expectations of others and enhances the smooth functioning of social and community life. For example, in our society we tend to present ourselves as healthy, happy, successful, and "cool" while, in reality, we may feel lousy, be depressed, and be worried about our next car payment.

In our private moments with a friend, however, we can "let our hair down," be more genuine, and share our concerns.

Throughout human history the persona, as an archetype, has held an important survival value for the individual by acknowledging the demands and expectations of the society.

Exercise 1

a. Identify and describe two major roles or social masks you assume as you go about your life.

Persona #1

Persona #2

b. Our persona may be in conflict with more genuine features of our personality. It is very important, therefore, to realize that the persona has significant dangers, as well as assets, for the personality. We may identify so strongly with our persona or social role that we lose touch with our uniqueness and individuality. We may, in other words, play the role so successfully that we fail to develop other, more authentic aspects of our personality. Is this a possibility for you? Have you become alienated from some important aspect of your personality owing to an overdeveloped persona? Discuss and illustrate.

The Shadow.   This archetype represents aspects of our personality we wish to hide from ourselves and others. The shadow is composed of any aspect of self that we are reluctant to face whether it is positive or negative. It is important for psychic health and wholeness to bring the shadow aspects of our personality into awareness so that we can work with them constructively. Jung considered the realization of the shadow to be an act of courage.

Exercise 2

Do any of your dreams, fantasies, behaviors, or other indications suggest the shadow side of your personality? Remember that the shadow is composed of both negative *and* positive features of personality you are reluctant to face. The latter, for example, may be represented by a hidden or denied talent.

The Anima and Animus.   The anima is the feminine side of the personality in males, and the animus represents the masculine aspects of personality in females. For the male, the anima archetype has developed out of thousands of years of experience with women: mothers, wives, lovers, and friends. The same holds true for its counterpart, the animus, in females.

Both the anima and the animus archetypes of the collective unconscious help us, male and female, to develop a more nearly complete understanding of ourselves and the opposite sex. Thus, to ensure harmonious and balanced living, the feminine side of the male's personality and the masculine side of the female's personality need to be conscious and free for appropriate development and expression. As males we need to recognize our feminine qualities, and as females we need to recognize our masculine qualities. If not, our lives will be one-dimensional, and our sexual identity may become more a persona than a richly integrated aspect of our personality.

Exercise 3

a. As a male, are you in touch with your anima, your "feminine" qualities, i.e., your "soft side," feelings, the artistic, the expressive and emotional? If so, identify and describe how the anima functions in your life and how it is expressed in your personality.

b. As a female, are you in touch with your animus, your "masculine" qualities, i.e., your "hard side," logic, strength, aggressiveness, and so forth? If so, identify and describe how the animus functions in your life and how it is currently expressed in your personality.

B. THE STRUCTURE OF CONSCIOUSNESS—THE BASIC ATTITUDES OF EXTRAVERSION AND INTROVERSION

We have considered some of the dynamics of the collective unconscious and its influence on personality development. Jung was also concerned with the structure, operation, and impact of consciousness on the personality.

He identified two primary attitudes, extraversion and introversion, that determine the orientation and direction of the conscious mind. Both are basic attitudes toward self and the world.

Extraversion. Extraversion is an attitude characterized by a direction of psychic energy outward, toward the objective world and away from the subjective. The extravert focuses attention outward upon people, objects, and the external environment. Extraverts tend to be sociable, friendly, open, and approachable. Again, as with all other aspects of Jung's theory, there is danger in one-sided development. The danger for extraverts, as Jung saw it, was getting "sucked into objects" and ignoring the important subjective side of personality.

Introversion. The introvert, on the other hand, is oriented toward the subjective where energy is focused toward inner psychic processes. He or she tends to be reserved and shy and defends self against people, external objects, and demands. The introvert will frequently ignore objective and external realities and favor subjective qualities and "inner data." The danger for the introvert is losing touch with people, with the objective, and getting lost in subjective concerns.

Exercise 4

As you appraise your basic attitude or orientation, do you consider yourself more of an extravert or an introvert? Remembering that none of us is completely extraverted or introverted, describe the role of both attitudes in your life. Is one attitude much more powerful than the other? If so, does this imbalance create certain negative consequences for you? Discuss.

Corrective Function of the Unconscious. Central to Jungian theory is the compensatory or corrective function of the unconscious. Any highly developed (and therefore conscious) aspect of personality has its opposite in the unconscious. The unconscious plays, therefore, a compensating role in pressing for the development of the recessed or neglected characteristic. If we become too "highly specialized" (too strongly introverted or extraverted, dominated by our persona, one-sided in our masculine or feminine features, etc.), the unconscious serves a vital corrective function by asserting itself through certain symptoms and behaviors. This compensatory dynamic of the unconscious functions to open the neglected area to consciousness and create greater flexibility and balance within the personality.

Exercise 5

Have you experienced some symptom or behavior that might represent a "message" from the unconscious to strengthen a neglected area of your personality? Describe the form the message took and how it enlightened you.

C. THE FOUR FUNCTIONS OF CONSCIOUSNESS—THINKING, FEELING, SENSING, AND INTUITING

Jung identified four primary psychological or mental functions: thinking, feeling, sensing, and intuiting. These four functions or types are our primary ways of perceiving the environment and integrating experiences.

The thinking type is focused on making judgments from a logical and rational process. For those of us in whom the thinking function predominates, there is concern for arriving at objective truth through logical analysis and other cognitive processes.

The feeling type is also concerned primarily with making judgments, not on the basis of objective and logical criteria, but on the basis of how one feels about something. The validity of an idea for the feeling type is, therefore, to be found in one's positive or negative feelings.

Both thinking and feeling are considered to be *rational functions* in that they are both concerned with making evaluations and judgments.

The sensation type places supreme importance on tangible experiences and sensations. Thus, this type is oriented to details within the environment (he/she will usually remember where the car is located in the parking lot) and to all concrete sensations such as touch, smell, taste, and visual stimulation.

The intuitive type relies heavily on past experience and unconscious processes. This type is inclined to operate on hunches and intuition, which may also involve extrasensory perception. Since neither sensation nor intuition requires a rational process, both are considered to be *irrational functions*.

Whereas most of us have developed one or two dominant functions, the goal of individuation is to develop some strength and flexibility in all four functions.

Exercise 6

a. On the basis of your self-experience, which type represents your *primary* or dominant function? Which type represents your weakest function? Present a brief description of each in your life.

b. Do you see any implications for your vocation or occupational choice in your dominant attitude (extraversion/introversion) and your dominant functions? Are these strengths represented in your plans? Discuss.

c. Is your dominant *attitude* and *function* a source of conflict as you interact with significant others who have developed different dominants? Discuss.

d. Are there ways of approaching this disharmony in one of your important relationships that would aid the individuation process for each of you? Please allow time to reflect on this question and discuss.

In Jung's typology each basic attitude is linked to a dominant function. For example, there is an extraverted–thinking type and an introverted–thinking type and so on. To pursue these relationships complicates matters beyond the scope of this workbook. If, however, you are interested in pursuing your special combination of attitude and function and its implications, speak to your teacher. He or she might arrange for you or your class to take the Myers-Briggs Type Indicator.

D. SUMMARY EXERCISE

What are some of the important things you have learned about yourself after doing these exercises on Jung's theory of personality? Which was the most valuable exercise for you. Why?

Classroom Exercise

Join a small discussion group and share with one another what you learned and found important in this unit. After 20 minutes come together as a whole class and discuss your major learnings.

Karen Horney and Psychoanalytical Social Theory

A. **Moving Toward Others, Moving Against Others, Moving Away From Others**
B. **Preconditions for Decision Making**
C. **The Tyranny of the Should**
D. **Cultural Influences on Personality**
E. **Masculine and Feminine Psychology**
F. **Summary Exercise**

When it comes to understanding the complexities of the neurotic personality and the process by which such distortions occur, Karen Horney has no peer. She spent her long and distinguished career studying and treating neurotic individuals. Fortunately, Horney was also a writer, and the richness of her clinical experience and the depth of her understanding of neurotic conflicts and the neurotic process are available to us through three primary works: *The Neurotic Personality of Our Time* (1973); *Our Inner Conflicts* (1945); and *Neurosis and Human Growth* (1950). In these works Horney details her theory of the neurotic condition. It is a theory that departs from the Freudian view by emphasizing the importance of interpersonal and cultural factors in personality development.

Although Horney focused on the development of the neurotic personality, she also deepened our understanding of the needs, conflicts, and coping strategies that we all share. She emphasized that " . . . the crucial conflicts around which a neurosis grows are practically always the same. In general, they are the same conflicts to which the healthy person in our culture is also subject" (1937, p. 281).

With this important idea in mind let us develop Horney's theoretical position before we proceed to the exercises.

If a child has favorable conditions for growth, if the child is loved, respected, and treated with consistency, he or she will grow toward *self-realization* and develop the feelings, wishes, strengths, and abilities that foster the development of the *real self*, that central force which is the source of all healthy growth.

If, on the other hand, the child is subjected to adverse influences (parents who are dominating, overprotective, intimidating, unable to fully love the child) they will have an adverse effect on the child's development. The child eventually develops a profound insecurity, with feelings of apprehension, distrust, and isolation. Horney refers to this condition in the child as one of *basic anxiety*.

A. MOVING TOWARD OTHERS, MOVING AGAINST OTHERS, MOVING AWAY FROM OTHERS

In order to cope with these feelings of being isolated and helpless in a hostile world, the child is driven by an inner necessity toward one of three neurotic trends: moving toward people, moving against people, and moving away from people. We can summarize these three trends as follows:

1. *Moving toward people — the compliant type — the appeal of love.* This neurotic direction involves a craving for affection and approval; the person needs to be desired, needed, protected, cared for; feels weak and helpless.
2. *Moving against people — the aggressive type — the appeal of mastery.* This neurotic direction involves a craving for power; the person assumes everyone is hostile; there is a strong need to exploit and outsmart others to achieve success and prestige.
3. *Moving away from people — the detached type — the appeal of freedom.* This direction involves a craving for freedom and detachment. There is a general estrangement from people and a need to put emotional distance between self and others. They draw a "magic circle" around themselves that no one can penetrate. They need to prove, through self-sufficiency, that they don't need others.

In the neurotic personality these three neurotic directions are unconscious, exaggerated, and maladaptive. In the normal person, however, they can function in an adaptive and flexible manner and are complementary, making for a "harmonious whole." Horney (1966) describes the flexible and adaptive character of the three directions as they function in the relatively healthy person.

> In moving toward people, the person tries to create for himself a friendly relation to his world. In moving against people, he equips himself for survival in a competitive society. In moving away from people, he hopes to attain a certain integrity and serenity. As a matter of fact, all three attitudes are not only desirable but necessary to our development as human beings. (p. 89)

The important distinction is that, in the neurotic orientation to life, these trends become compulsive, rigid, indiscriminate, and eventually exclusive. In neurotic persons, for example, their very existence, happiness, and security depend upon the need for love, for power, or for freedom and isolation. Although one of these trends will eventually dominate the development of the personality, the *central neurotic conflict* lies in the fact that the neurotic, like all of us, has a need for a balanced satisfaction in all three areas, and he or she cannot achieve this.

Exercise 1

a. How do you experience each of these trends? Describe how each trend functions in your life and provide examples to illustrate the role of each trend in your personality.

Moving toward others

Moving against others

Moving away from others

b. Do you find that one of the three trends tends to assume a more dominant position in your life? Describe your *prevailing trend* and discuss both its assets (how does the dominant trend enhance your development?) and its liabilities (how does the dominant trend interfere with your development?).

c. What steps might you take to create a more harmonious relationship among the three trends?

B. PRECONDITIONS FOR DECISION MAKING

Karen Horney emphasizes that it is both the prerogative and the burden of human beings to make decisions. In doing so, we are often torn between contradictory needs, wishes, and impulses. We may want to be alone but also with a friend; we may want to major in art and also want to study medicine; or we may be in a conflict between obligation and desire. Horney also emphasizes in this connection that it is not neurotic to have such conflicts. But the more we are unaware of our inner conflicts or those we have with our society, the less we are able to recognize the contradictory issues in our lives that must be considered if we are to make good choices and decisions.

Horney discusses four important preconditions for healthy, productive decision making. These preconditions may help you identify some of the underlying issues in your difficulties with decision making.

1. We must be aware of our real wishes and feelings.
2. We must have developed our own set of values. They must be *our* values and not values that we have merely adopted from our parents or environment.
3. Even if we are confident in our feelings and values and clearly recognize a conflict, we must be able to renounce one of the two contradictory possibilities. That is, we must make a conscious choice to deny one option and affirm the other.
4. We must be willing to take responsibility for our decision.

Exercise 2

a. Select an important decision you have made in the past. Describe the process you went through and the difficulties you faced in making that decision. In the light of Horney's four preconditions for decision making, which one of these preconditions caused you the greatest difficulty in making your decision? Discuss.

b. Identify an important and/or difficult decision you are working on now or are anticipating in the near future. In the following exercise, try to clarify some of the issues you face in making this decision by considering each of Horney's preconditions for decision making.

1. Briefly describe the decision you face and try to identify your real *wishes* and gut *feelings* regarding this decision.

2. Construct a hierarchy of your values. List, in order of importance, the things that matter to *you* the most. Consider such things as the time, attention, and energy you devote to various areas of your life. How might your hierarchy of values enter into the decision you must make?

3. Is this examination of your real wishes, feelings, and values helpful to you in confirming one option and renouncing the other? Discuss.

4. Will it be difficult for you to take responsibility for the decision you make? What are the issues for you here? What frightens you the most?

c. Has this process of examining your decision in the light of Horney's preconditions for healthy decision making been of help to you? Has it helped clarify an important issue for you? Discuss.

C. THE TYRANNY OF THE SHOULD

Horney points out that the neurotic's life is dictated by what she calls the "tyranny of the should." That is, the neurotic person structures much of life and personality around what he or she "should" be like instead of responding to genuine needs, desires, feelings, etc. For example: "I *should* never make mistakes" or "I *should* be liked by everyone." By following the dictates of the "should," the individual moves away from the *real self* and structures a pseudo-self built around false expectations, ideals, and goals and thus creates an idealized image of the self. Eventually, these inner dictates (the "shoulds") move the personality from "I *should* be this kind of person" to "I *am* this kind of person." Thus, a false self is constructed and protected.

The tyranny of the should not only is a serious problem for the neurotic personality but also, at times, becomes a negative force for each of us.

Exercise 3

a. Try to identify some of the important "shoulds" in your life that you have created in order to enhance or protect your self-image. List the dominant "shoulds" that currently operate in your life.

b. Do you have any ideas about the source of your "shoulds," that is, family, society, or others?

c. Horney points out that living by a set of "shoulds" impairs our spontaneity and often produces a feeling of being cramped, tense, or hemmed in. It may also impair interpersonal relationships by making us demand too much of others, i.e., projecting our "shoulds" onto others.

Select one of your most tyrannical "shoulds" and try to identify what difficulties it is causing you.

d. How would you be a different person if you gave up the tyranny of this "should" in your life? Discuss.

D. CULTURAL INFLUENCES ON PERSONALITY

One of the important ways in which Karen Horney helped transform psychoanalytic theory was in her recognition of the importance of social and cultural factors in fostering neurotic developments in the personality. Whereas Freud viewed culture as the sublimated expressions of sexual and aggressive drives, Horney saw cultural values and practices as being a major factor in the formation and reinforcement of neurotic maladaptive behavior.

She recognized that there are typical difficulties inherent in our culture that "mirror" themselves as conflicts in every individual's life and that often lead to the formation of a neurosis.

Horney identified the following conditions in our dominant culture that create problems for all of us and that are strongly implicated in the formation of neurosis.

- The irrational quest for possessions that is falsely associated with satisfying our need for security, power, and self-esteem
- A destructive competition and rivalry that radiates from an economic center into all areas of our life and impairs love, social relationships, school life, and play
- An exaggerated need for love, with the unrealistic expectation that love will resolve all the conflicts to which we are heir in our society

Exercise 4

How have you experienced, and been influenced by, these neurotic characteristics of our culture? Have they helped create certain conflicts and tensions in your life? Be as specific as possible and discuss their impact on you. In doing this exercise, it may be helpful to reflect on your responses to the exercises in section C above.

E. MASCULINE AND FEMININE PSYCHOLOGY

One of Karen Horney's important contributions involves her reinterpretation of Freud's account of male–female development. She was highly critical of the traditional psychoanalytic view, for example, that females were locked into a perpetual desire for a penis (penis envy), which represented a "superior endowment" for development. In Freud's view, promoted in much of the psychoanalytic literature, these phallic needs and strivings inevitably doomed the girl to feelings of deficiency and inferiority, often resulting in actual inferiority.

While not discounting the possibility of penis envy as a developmental stage in the young girl, Horney rejects the Freudian notion that "anatomy is destiny," that early penis envy accounts for the female's "masculine complex" and an underlying feeling of inadequacy and inferiority vis-à-vis male development. Instead, Horney felt that these unfortunate developments in the female personality were due largely to social forces and a predominantly masculine psychology. "In actual fact," observes Horney (1973), "a girl is exposed from birth onward to the suggestion—inevitably, whether conveyed brutally or delicately—of her inferiority, an experience that constantly stimulates her masculine complex" (p. 69).

Owing to the masculine character of our civilization and the traditional dogma of woman's inferiority, Horney observed that men are under a greater necessity, often unconscious, to depreciate women than conversely.

Horney (1937) observed that "while men grew up with the conviction that they had to achieve something in life if they wanted to get somewhere, women realized that through love, and love alone, could they attain happiness, security, and prestige" (p. 190).

Horney believed that this distinction has had a great impact on the psychic position of males and females and has resulted in the woman's quest for love (overvaluation of love) as a major source for security and happiness.

Exercise 5

a. As a *male*, are you in touch with any tendencies in yourself to depreciate the female? That is, do you stereotype the female, or think of them as less able, or assign them to a "female" role, and so forth? Try to be as self-searching and as honest as you can as you think about Horney's observations.

b. What is your idea of the "ideal" woman?

c. As a *female*, have you *felt* depreciated by the male? Have you encountered specific instances of such attitudes or treatment by a male or males that would support Horney's claim? Discuss.

d. As a female, do you feel, at times, that you fit Horney's picture, that you shy away from independence and achievement in favor of love? Discuss your experience and how this "need" for love has influenced or might influence your goals and plans for the future.

F. SUMMARY EXERCISE

What are some of the important things you have learned about yourself after doing these exercises on Horney's theory of personality? Which was the most valuable exercise for you? Why?

Classroom Exercise

Join a small discussion group and share with one another what you learned and found important in this unit. After 20 minutes come together as a whole class and discuss your major learnings.

Erik Erikson
and
Psychosocial Theory

A. The First Three Psychosocial Stages
B. Psychosocial Stage Four: Industry versus Inferiority
C. Psychosocial Stage Five: Adolescence— Ego Identity versus Role Confusion
D. Psychosocial Stage Six: Young Adulthood—Intimacy versus Isolation
E. Psychosocial Stage Seven: Middle Adulthood— Generativity versus Stagnation
F. Psychosocial Stage Eight: Old Age— Integrity versus Despair
G. Summary Exercise

Healthy growth of the personality, according to Erikson, depends upon the successful resolution of eight "phase specific" stages in ego development throughout the life span. Each stage unfolds in a biologically predetermined sequence in interaction with social forces and the requirements of the culture, and each represents a critical period of transition in the healthy development of the ego and evolution of the personality. As one follows this epigenetic principle of maturation, the healthy resolution of a given stage of development depends in large measure upon the strength of the foundation established in the earlier stages. Each stage becomes a crucial building block in the developmental process and ego functioning.

The contributions of Erik Erikson to personality theory are considerable. He recognized (as Freud did not) the ego as an autonomous personality structure interacting with social and historical forces. He also discovered the importance of ego development throughout the life cycle.

A. THE FIRST THREE PSYCHOSOCIAL STAGES

The first two stages in Erikson's theory of ego development are the development of *basic trust* (birth to year one) and the attainment of a *sense of autonomy* (second and third years).

Basic trust, for Erikson the cornerstone of a healthy personality, must be established early in the child's life or a pattern of mistrust—a lack of confidence and hope—develops. To establish basic trust in one's self and the world, the infant, during this oral period, must experience reliability and consistency in the environment.

Failure to develop autonomy in the second psychosocial stage will lead to shame and self-doubt. This task parallels Freud's anal stage and relates in part to the child's development of personal control during toilet training.

Erikson's third stage of psychosocial development is the acquiring of a sense of initiative versus a sense of guilt (ages 4 to 6). This is a period of heightened identification with parents as the child struggles to explore the kind of person he or she is going to become. Increased motor control and locomotion, language development, and imagination become important personal resources for this crucial exploration. There is also experimentation with a growing sexuality. Play becomes especially important during this period and may be related to the resolution of Oedipal conflict and guilt and to a working through of the conflicts of taking the initiative and planning for projects in the "real" world.

Play also enables the child, through imagination and fantasy, to anticipate and experiment with future developments in the personality. In play the child has the opportunity to create dramatic versions of an inner and outer world, to experiment with roles and relationships within the relative safety of play and fantasy.

B. PSYCHOSOCIAL STAGE FOUR: INDUSTRY VERSUS INFERIORITY

In the fourth stage of Erikson's eight stages of psychosocial development, the basic struggle in ego development becomes one of *industry versus inferiority*. It is during this stage (about 6 to 11 years of age and corresponding to Freud's latent period) that ego maturity crystallizes around the conviction that "I am what I learn." Thus, healthy ego maturity during this stage is based in large measure on learning the skills and competencies of the culture. An early frustrating and/or unsuccessful experience in school may produce feelings of inadequacy and inferiority. The ego strength to be achieved during this psychosocial stage is *competence*.

Exercise 1

a. Think back to your early years in school. Was this a discouraging and frustrating time for you, or were you able to achieve success in learning and in developing the skills necessary to experience an important sense of industry and competence? Did you have special difficulty in learning to read, doing numbers and math, writing, or spelling? Discuss your school experiences at this fourth stage of psychosocial maturity and evaluate your development. Was a certain teacher important to your success or failure?

b. Perhaps there were other resources and skill developments *outside* the school setting that offered you important opportunities to gratify your need for this ego development. For example, did a parent, grandparent, or family friend substitute in some ways or compensate for school difficulties to provide other opportunities for competence and skill development for you? Even if your early school experiences were successful, these additional opportunities might have been very important to you. Discuss.

c. What *specific* learning, competence, or skill development do you remember as being the *most important* to you in gratifying your need for a feeling of industry and competence? This may or may not relate to formal school learning for you. Briefly discuss its role in your ego development.

C. PSYCHOSOCIAL STAGE FIVE:
ADOLESCENCE—EGO IDENTITY VERSUS ROLE CONFUSION

Adolescence is a developmental period marked by much confusion and uncertainty. It is a time of searching for stability and continuity in the personality.

One of Erikson's major contributions to personality theory is his theoretical analysis of the identity problems that young people encounter during adolescence. The well-known term *identity crisis* comes from his work.

As a college student you are moving toward the end of this period of development known as adolescence (approximately age 12 to 21). In Erikson's view the major task for this period of development is to achieve a stable ego identity versus possible role confusion and crisis in identity formation. The ego strength to be achieved during this psychosocial stage is *fidelity*.

There are many aspects to achieving a stable ego identity. Values clarification, developing preferences, and identifying continuity in one's life are among the important contributions. Erikson also stressed the importance of occupational identity to the resolution of stage five.

In his monograph *Identity and the Life Cycle*, Erikson (1959) states, for example, that "in general it is primarily the inability to settle on an occupational identity which disturbs young people" (p. 92).

Exercise 2

a. In your own efforts to establish a stable ego identity, has your quest for and confusion over an occupational identity been a major concern and disturbance for you? Discuss your experience.

b. Have you now established a satisfying occupational identity? If so, has this achievement been of major importance to you in your overall stability and ego identity formation? Discuss.

Exercise 3

As you know, we are living in a time of changing sex roles and patterns, and there is much sex-role confusion in our society. Have these social changes contributed to your personal difficulties in achieving a stable ego identity? Discuss this from your personal orientation and experiences as a male or female.

Exercise 4

a. In an effort to find ego support and stability through the adolescent years, young people frequently turn to (idolize) one or more heroes of the popular culture (TV star, rock star, athlete, and so forth). Was there an important "hero" in your life who contributed to your own sense of identity? Name the most important "hero" for you during your adolescence and discuss his or her value to you in your struggle to establish a stable ego identity. What characteristics of this "hero" were important to you? What ego needs were you trying to meet through this identification?

b. Erikson has stressed that *overidentification* with a popular hero may actually limit the development of one's ego identity rather than enhance it. Have you experienced such an overidentification with a hero? If so, do you agree with Erikson that it was detrimental in some ways to your own ego identity formation? Discuss. If you have not experienced such an overidentification, have you had a friend whose overidentification with his or her hero illustrates Erikson's caution?

Exercise 5

Before leaving our work on Erikson's fifth stage of psychosocial development, per-haps it would be helpful for you to develop a summary appraisal of the degree to which you feel you have achieved a stable ego identity. In this appraisal discuss the *strengths* you have developed and the *tasks* yet to be completed.

D. PSYCHOSOCIAL STAGE SIX:
YOUNG ADULTHOOD—INTIMACY VERSUS ISOLATION

While you are in the process of moving out of the adolescent period of development, you are also moving rapidly into Erikson's sixth stage of ego maturity, young adulthood. We might say that you are in the awkward position of having one foot in adolescence and the other in young adulthood. This can be a difficult transition.

The crisis of this new developmental period will be in achieving *intimacy versus isolation*. This task of emerging adulthood is different from all previous psychosocial stages. Prior to this time, you were concerned with your own ego and its enhancement. In young adulthood, however, your challenge is to bring your ego into fusion with another, to establish a genuine intimacy with another person. In some respects, this requires the merging of one's identity with another. This can be accomplished, Erikson insists, only if at the time of the potential intimacy and fusion you have achieved a sufficient degree of "intimacy" with yourself. That is, you must be sufficiently strong in your own sense of ego identity that you will not fear giving something of yourself in an intimate relationship.

The crucial question becomes: Am I strong enough in my identity to fuse myself with another without the fear of losing my own identity, autonomy, and integrity? It is not until this strength of ego identity is attained, says Erikson, that we are capable of mature love and intimacy. The ego strength to be achieved during this psychosocial stage is *love*.

Exercise 6

Perhaps you have attained a sufficient sense of ego identity to have already experienced, or to be ready for, a deep and satisfying intimacy with another person. Perhaps not. In any case, appraise your current readiness for intimacy and fusion with another person and briefly discuss a relationship you had or presently have that illustrates your appraisal.

E. PSYCHOSOCIAL STAGE SEVEN:
MIDDLE ADULTHOOD—GENERATIVITY VERSUS STAGNATION

In the final three developmental stages of ego development we move away from the "self" to the "other," to a more interpersonal and social orientation. Following the resolution of the adolescent identity crisis in stage five there is, in stage six, the task of developing love and intimacy. In stage seven, the focus of the present exercise, there is an advancement in ego maturity that is realized through the "need to be needed." The middle years of life (approximately 25 to 55) are focused on the developmental crisis of generativity versus stagnation. One's identity is sustained and enhanced through the development of generativity and the resulting ego strength of *care*.

Generativity, for Erikson, is primarily the interest in and commitment to establishing and guiding the next generation. As an instinctual force, however, generativity is not limited to procreation and the care of children but extends to whatever a person may generate, create, produce, and leave behind as a foundation for the next generation. It expresses a "belief in the species." Generativity may, therefore, express itself in concern for the environment, in teaching, historical preservation, and supporting the arts, and other pursuits.

A failure to resolve this developmental issue in favor of generativity leaves the person self-absorbed and with a feeling of stagnation, boredom, and interpersonal impoverishment.

It will be a number of years before you face the developmental issue of generativity versus self-centeredness and stagnation. Your parents may now, however, be engaged in working through the tensions of this psychosocial stage of ego development. This exercise will give you an opportunity to appraise their current development from this perspective.

Exercise 7

How are your mother and father each expressing and developing ego maturity through generativity? Now that most of the children are grown, do you see this as a difficult and frustrating stage for them? Consider your parents' development from the perspective of this psychosocial stage and discuss your observations.

F. PSYCHOSOCIAL STAGE EIGHT:
OLD AGE—INTEGRITY VERSUS DESPAIR

With the coming of old age the person enters the final psychosocial stage of ego development and maturity. This stage represents a philosophical appraisal and "summing-up" of one's life and its meaning. In its healthy manifestation it represents the fruits of the past seven stages and is expressed as an acceptance of one's life cycle in all of its aspects, including achievements, successes, failures, weaknesses and strengths, and relationships. One feels the significance and dignity of one's life, and death is no longer feared. The ego strength to be achieved during this psychosocial stage is *wisdom*.

The failure to achieve this final ego integration is expressed in despair, depression, and sense of failure and disgust. There is frequently an obsession over unfulfilled promises and missed opportunities.

Exercise 8

Your grandparents are involved in this final stage of ego affirmation. As you look at their lives, do you see the development of integrity or despair and disgust? Discuss your observations of your grandparents' resolution of this final stage of ego maturity.

G. SUMMARY EXERCISE

What are some of the important things you have learned about yourself after doing these exercises on Erikson's psychosocial theory? Which was the most valuable exercise for you? Why?

Classroom Exercise

Join a small discussion group and share with one another what you learned and found important in this unit. After 20 minutes come together as a whole class and discuss your major learnings.

Albert Bandura
and
Social Learning
Theory

A. Learning Through Observation and
   Modeling
B. Self-Reinforcement
C. Self-Management: Controlling Your
   Own Behavior
D. Perceived Self-Efficacy
E. Summary Exercise

Albert Bandura has played a leading role in the demise of a half-century of the behaviorist tradition in American psychology. While Bandura's orientation is identified within this tradition, his social–cognitive theories have, nevertheless, transformed the simplistic views of personality development presented by B. F. Skinner and other classical behaviorists. These one-dimensional views, stressing the importance of environmental reinforcement while rejecting the validity of internal variables, have been largely abandoned.

Respecting the complexity of human personality and behavior, Bandura has focused his attention on symbolic processes and the potential for self-reinforcement and self-regulation. His model of *reciprocal determinism* includes, therefore, the interaction and integration of three crucial variables: *behavior, personal variables*, and *environmental events*.

According to Bandura, neither internal variables nor environmental forces alone are responsible for personality development. It is the *interaction* of these variables and the individual's capacity to integrate them that is at the heart of Bandura's theory.

All of these interactional processes leading to self-directed behavior are centered on the carefully researched concepts of *observational learning* and *modeling*. In this unit you will explore the significance of these and other contributions by Bandura.

A. LEARNING THROUGH OBSERVATION AND MODELING

According to Bandura, as we have seen, most human behavior is not a simple result of the rewards (reinforcements) and punishments that immediately follow behavior as in B. F. Skinner's operant conditioning. Instead, our behavioral repertoire develops through a complex process of observational learning and modeling. Bandura places importance on our cognitive skills in this learning process and on our ability to modify our own behavior. Bandura remains true to the principles of reinforcement, but he believes that many of our behaviors and expectations are learned indirectly by observing another's actions and the consequences they bring about.

Exercise 1

Identify and discuss an important value, habit, or other personality characteristic that you feel you have acquired or developed through observational learning and modeling. Specify the individual (the model) and some specific situations that have influenced you in this learning.

Exercise 2

a. Social learning theory suggests that patterns of emotional expression may also develop as a consequence of observational learning and modeling. Two important areas of emotional expression and behavior within the family are anger and love. Discuss the specific ways in which your parents express these emotions. For example, how do they express conflict? Do they touch and hug?

b. Do you feel that social learning theory offers an explanation for your present ways of expressing love and anger; i.e., have you modeled these expressions from your parents' behavior?

Exercise 3

a. Bandura's research indicates that television is an important source of observational learning and modeling for the child. What were your two favorite television programs as a child? Was there a favorite character or personality in each of these programs with whom you identified?

b. Was an attitude or behavior influenced by these programs in any way that would indicate learning through modeling? Discuss.

c. As adults we are also vulnerable to the influence of television. For example, one researcher has recently suggested that the characterizations on popular TV shows could contribute to anorexia among young women who have TV stars (young and thin) as role models. In what ways do you feel you have been influenced by the current values, behaviors, images, etc. presented to you on TV?

B. SELF-REINFORCEMENT

Bandura has identified an additional source of reinforcement in the control and modification of behavior. This is the reinforcement that one creates for oneself after one's standards of achievement are realized. In other words, we often select or create our own incentives and do not merely respond in a mechanical fashion to external rewards and punishments, as operant conditioning suggests. Feeling a sense of pride in a job well done is an example of this self-reinforcement.

Exercise 4

Present two current examples of self-reinforcement that stimulate, motivate, or sustain your behavior. Identify the behavior in each example and the self-evaluative reactions it generates for you.

C. SELF-MANAGEMENT: CONTROLLING YOUR OWN BEHAVIOR

Among the promising applications of Bandura's theoretical work are the techniques that have been developed to help us control and alter our own behavior. The capacity for self-influence fosters personal control and self-directedness. This is done primarily by evaluating one's behavior, eliminating or altering intrusive environmental factors, and planning a sound personal schedule of positive incentives for our desired behavior. These three elements in a self-management program illustrate Bandura's principle of reciprocal determinism: an integration of both inner and outer controls.

Williams and Long (1979), in their book *Toward a Self-Managed Life Style*, outline five major steps in initiating any self-management program. Before you embark upon the self-management program suggested in this workbook, it will be helpful for you to become acquainted with Williams and Long's suggestions. Their five major steps in a self-management program are summarized here.*

1. *Selecting a goal.* This is a crucial stage. Your goal should be important to you. You need to be highly motivated to change the behavior. Otherwise, no techniques are likely to work. You should also be able to translate the goal into measurable behavioral terms, such as the ability to identify specific behaviors and record

---

*Adapted with permission from the publisher, Houghton Mifflin Company.

them. For example, if you want to stop smoking, the goal can be readily identified and progress can be measured by the number of cigarettes you eliminate each day or week.

2. *Monitoring your target behavior.* It is important to keep an exact record of your *present behavior* (how many cigarettes you are smoking, how many hours you are studying each day, and so forth) for a period of time in order to establish a baseline reference point from which to measure your progress. A careful record of your progress throughout the program should also be kept. A record of environmental factors that contribute to your unwanted behavior is also important, for you will want to alter some of these factors.

3. *Changing settings.* You may need to alter aspects of your environment in order to control situations that encourage your undesired behavior. Avoiding a bakery shop redolent of hot cookies and doughnuts is an example of controlling the setting that encourages high caloric intake.

4. *Establishing effective consequences.* Here we come to one of the major Bandurian principles: The management and control of behavior through self-chosen incentives. This is the art and science of planning for rewards contingent upon your desired behavior. It is self-evident that your plan must include incentives that are really motivating and rewarding for you.

5. *Consolidating gains.* This final step involves gradually giving up your need for many of the artificial supports so that the desirable behavior functions automatically, providing its own satisfying consequences. Reach this level gradually, Williams and Long suggest, and retain as many naturally supporting elements in your environment as possible. (pp. 25–26)

Exercise 5

a. This exercise asks you to plan and implement a self-management program, not only to experience directly some important aspects of Bandura's principle of reciprocal determinism, but also to add to your own self-confidence. One aspect of your present life that you might wish to alter is your study behavior. Following the steps suggested by Williams and Long (1979), plan a self-managed alteration of your study habits. (If your study behavior is satisfactory for you, choose some other undesirable habit or behavior, such as smoking or bad money management.)

- Be as specific and as clear as possible in identifying your goal. What, specifically, do you want to change about your study habits or pattern of behavior? For example, do you want to increase the length of study time for each day, increase the length of each individual study period, decrease interruptions, or what?
- Keep a record for one week of your *current* study habits (or smoking, or whatever), including the exact times you study and the exact conditions under which you study. Use the baseline data sheet provided on page 80 for this purpose.
- Alter the situations that contribute to your inefficient study behavior. For example, you might go to the library each night instead of suffering the interruptions of studying in your room.
- Once you have altered your environment and established a reasonable study schedule, introduce an attractive incentive program into your schedule. Build in some rewarding experience to follow the successful completion of the desired study behavior.

- Maintain this schedule until your new study behavior becomes "second nature" and as habitual as your previous behavior was.

  Important: Having established your baseline behavior, keep a record of your progress throughout the program.

  Consider and respond to the following items before beginning your project.

1. An objective analysis of my present study behavior (smoking behavior, etc.)

2. Specific goals for my project to alter my study behavior

3. Environmental changes I will need to make

4. My incentive plan to reward my improved study behavior (Be sure that your reward system follows good reinforcement principles.)

   b. Describe your experience and evaluate the results of your personal program for self-directed change. Did you find Bandura's approach helpful in altering some aspect of your behavior? Discuss.

BASE-LINE STUDY BEHAVIOR

7:00 A.M	4:00 P.M.
8:00 A.M.	5:00 P.M.
9:00 A.M.	6:00 P.M.
10:00 A.M.	7:00 P.M.
11:00 A.M.	8:00 P.M.
12:00 noon	9:00 P.M.
1:00 P.M.	10:00 P.M.
2:00 P.M.	11:00 P.M.
3:00 P.M.	12:00 midnight

Note: Make a copy of this chart for each day of the week. If you are trying to change a behavior other than studying, cross out "Study" in the title and insert the correct behavior.

D. PERCEIVED SELF-EFFICACY

Bandura has demonstrated that both goal setting and goal attainment are requirements in bringing about self-directed change. He has also shown that the effectiveness of goals and skills depends in large measure on one's belief in one's ability to pursue a goal successfully. The degree to which one has this self-confident belief or expectation of achievement is what Bandura calls perceived self-efficacy.

Exercise 6

a. Are you aware of the principle of perceived self-efficacy as it functions in your life to hinder or enhance your success in reaching goals? Illustrate the impact that a low degree of self-confidence has had on your ability or motivation to achieve a goal. Discuss your experience.

b. Illustrate the impact that a high degree of perceived self-efficacy has had on your success in reaching a goal. Discuss your experience.

c. Bandura's principle of perceived self-efficacy, the confidence one feels in reaching a goal, suggests an important variable in determining success, failure, or mediocre performance in college.

If you are not doing as well as you would like, or if your motivation for academic achievement is low, perhaps this is due to your lack of confidence in your ability to achieve higher goals.

Consider your academic goals and expectations and how your motivation, performance, and success are related to the internal variable of perceived self-efficacy. Discuss.

E. SUMMARY EXERCISE

What are some of the important things you have learned about yourself after doing these exercises on Bandura's social learning theory? Which was the most valuable exercise for you? Why?

Classroom Exercise

Join a small discussion group and share with one another what you learned and found important in this unit. After 20 to 30 minutes come together as a whole class and discuss your major learnings.

Gordon Allport
and
Trait Theory

Gordon Allport's theory focuses on the uniqueness of personality and on the healthy trends in human development. In all of his work he distinguishes between the peripheral and coping aspects of personality and those unique features of personality that are vital and central in the life of the individual for healthy development and maturity.

Allport believed that too much attention was devoted to understanding pathology in personality, and he considered attempts to construct a general psychology (applicable to all people) from neurotic potentials and trends, as in psychoanalytic formulations, to be totally invalid. In other words, the principles and concepts of development that are valid in understanding the neurotic personality are *not* applicable in understanding the healthy, mature personality.

This principle of discontinuity, a major theme throughout Allport's works, is seen most vividly in his concept of the *functional autonomy of motives*, where, in healthy development, one's motives are current, conscious, future oriented, and not tied to the past. Thus, Allport believed that in the healthy personality, motives tend to be conscious rather than unconscious.

For Allport, every individual represents a unique organization of traits and themes, and he championed the scientific study of the *individual* personality, the single case, to better understand the principles operating in uniqueness of personality and the formation of healthy trends. To this end, he pioneered in the analysis of personal documents, self-reports, and the study of the expressive behavior of the individual.

Although Allport is identified as a trait theorist and was America's first personality theorist, his broad social concerns led him into the exploration of such topics as values, religion, prejudice, and the psychology of rumor. For these studies, we might also regard Gordon Allport as one of our pioneers in social psychology.

We can readily see that Allport, unlike Freud, was an optimist in his belief in the human potential for healthy, creative living. The following unit will give you an opportunity to view your own development from Allport's optimistic perspective.

A. TRAIT THEORY

Allport was committed to a trait theory of personality. While he recognized the pervasiveness of *common traits*, that is, traits that most people in a given culture are likely to exhibit, he was more concerned with the traits of personality that were expressions of individuality and uniqueness. Allport referred to these traits as *individual traits* or *personal dispositions*.

Exercise 1

Viewing yourself, first, as a personality reflecting the primary values and characteristics of your culture, identify two of your *common traits* that most other people in our culture also exhibit to some degree. Show you express these two common traits and indicate how important they are as aspects of your personality.

The Three Dispositions.   Allport categorized the personal dispositions according to their strength or dominance in the person's life. He identified (1) the cardinal disposition, (2) central dispositions, and (3) secondary dispositions.

In an individual who has a *cardinal disposition*, almost every aspect of his or her personality is influenced by it. The individual's entire identity is shaped by this powerful disposition. We often label people who have a cardinal trait with names or words derived from historical or fictional characters, such as Christlike, quixotic, a scrooge, or a Don Juan.

Ordinarily, however, the personality develops around several outstanding features. These *central dispositions* form the dominant characteristics and trends of the personality, and Allport suggests that these central characteristics of personality are likely to be those we would mention in writing a letter of recommendation for someone.

Secondary dispositions, on the other hand, function more on the periphery of the personality. They are less significant, less conspicuous, and less consistent than the central dispositions.

Exercise 2

In this exercise you will be identifying the personal dispositions that are central in your own personality.

a. First, identify and briefly describe your cardinal disposition. (If your life is not dominated by a "ruling passion," or cardinal trait, describe the cardinal disposition of a friend or acquaintance.)

b. Consider your central dispositions. Identify the most significant central traits in your personality and *illustrate the recent functioning of each one*. Remember that central traits are the primary characteristics around which much of your personality is organized. (In a study by Allport, the average number of central traits listed by a group of college students was seven. Can you identify this many in your personality?)

c. Have someone who knows you well make an independent list of your central characteristics. How do they compare with your own list? How do you feel about your friend's list? Are there any surprises? You may find it helpful to discuss these with your friend.

B. FUNCTIONAL AUTONOMY OF MOTIVES

The principle of the *functional autonomy* of motives represents a radical departure from the Freudian view of motivation and is one of Allport's major contributions to personality theory. By this principle Allport meant that one's current motives have become independent (functionally autonomous) from the motivational forces and experiences of the past that may have originally helped form or create them. Thus, many of your motives today have a different meaning and purpose than they once had. Allport (1961) offers this analogy: "The life of a tree is continuous with that of its seed, but the seed no longer sustains and nourishes the full-grown tree" (p. 227).

Exercise 3

a. Your textbook (or instructor) has probably presented some good examples of the functional autonomy of motives. If you now understand this theory, try to discover an important example of the functional autonomy of motives in your own development. First, identify the original motive (usually formed in childhood) and its meaning and significance to you then.

b. Trace the development of this motive in your life as it became functionally autonomous. Show what meaning and purpose is *currently active* in the motive as it continues to function in your life.

C. EXPRESSIVE MOVEMENT AND BEHAVIOR

Allport gave serious attention to the unique features of the personality, and he was interested in studying aspects of the personality that reflected this uniqueness and individuality. Allport was interested, therefore, in all forms of *expressive behavior*, including handwriting, doodles, gestures, and gait. He believed that these expressive feature were *infallible* signatures of the person's unique style and individuality. Thus, Allport made an early contribution to the current interest in body language and nonverbal behavior.

Allport contrasted these expressive behaviors with *coping behavior*. These latter behaviors are more external to the individual, designed to alter and control the environment and to meet the conscious needs of the moment. Coping behavior, Allport emphasized, is task oriented and reflects a large degree of cultural conditioning.

Expressive behaviors, on the other hand, are more unconscious in their expression. They are more purposeless and spontaneous, revealing deeper personality structures and traits of the individual that are not expressed in coping behavior. In short, they are the more creative expressions of your personality.

Exercise 4

What style, movement, or behavior of yours is significant in expressing some important feature of your personality? Identify the expressive behavior and how it communicates some facet of your personality. A close friend or your roommate may have some observations that would be helpful to you in responding to this exercise.

Exercise 5

    a. Study the expressive behavior of one of your professors during two or more lectures or class periods. Try to distinguish between the coping aspects of his or her behavior and the style and behaviors that represent the more expressive components of the personality. Identify and describe the expressive behavior of your teacher. Do not mention names.

    b. After identifying the expressive components in your teacher's behavior, what do you infer about his or her personality?

Exercise 6

a. For several days try to be alert to the expressive behavior of gait. Observe different walking styles, their individuality and uniqueness. Select the gait of one person for closer observation and try to determine the possible meaning revealed in this person's expressive gait. Record your observations and inferences.

b. Does your own gait serve as a special expressive behavior?

D. HEALTHY PERSONALITY

Allport was more interested in the healthy, positive developments in the personality than in the immature and neurotic trends. He maintained that there is a qualitative difference (not just a matter of degree) between the neurotic personality and the healthy, mature one. In healthy development there is a growing maturity of propriate functions, those characteristics we regard as central and vital to our personality, and an increasing freedom from one's past (functional autonomy).

Allport listed and described six characteristics of the healthy or mature personality; these are summarized below.

1. *Extension of the sense of self.* The mature person has extended the boundaries of the self to a significant degree. The welfare of others becomes important to him or her. New interests, new skills, new ideas, and vocational direction all become incorporated into an expanding sense of self. There is a wider participation in life and a movement away from one's own ego and its protection.

2. *Warm relating of self to others.* There is a growing intimacy with others, and the mature person has developed the capacity to love. There is warmth and compassion, a concern and respect for others. This person wants to give love as much as to receive it.

3. *Emotional security (self-acceptance).* The mature personality has developed emotional poise and self-acceptance. There is a minimum of internal conflict, and frustration tolerance is very strong.

4. *Realistic perceptions and skills.* There is a growing ability to deal with reality. The mature personality displays a high degree of efficiency and accuracy of perception. Needs and fantasies do not distort the mature person's perceptions and judgments. There is a capacity for work and for the pursuit of projects outside the narrow confines of the ego. These individuals are problem centered rather than ego centered.

5. *Self-objectification: insight and humor.* Mature personalities have acquired a high degree of self-insight. They know themselves well and can be objective and accepting about most aspects of their personality. Accompanying this self-knowledge and objectivity is a sense of humor. Mature persons can laugh at themselves. This sense of humor is not based on hostility or the need to ridicule and put others down. Rather, it is based on a recognition of the common foibles inherent in the human condition and nonhostile sense of the comic in life.

6. *A unifying philosophy of life.* In the mature personality there is a sense of purpose and a "directedness" to life. The mature person has a firm underlying philosophy of life and a feeling that there is something very special to live for. Energy is directed toward a major goal.

Exercise 7

a. After reading and thinking about Allport's characteristics of the mature personality, evaluate your own present stage of development and maturity. Focus on those attributes you possess, as well as those you have yet to achieve. This is a good way to learn more about Allport and to give yourself some "gentle" feedback — maybe even to set some personal agenda for change.

1. Extension of the sense of self

2. Warm relating of self to others

3. Emotional security (self-acceptance)

4. Realistic perceptions and skills

5. Self-objectification: insight and humor

6. A unifying philosophy of life

    b. Which characteristic of the mature personality would you consider to be the most highly developed at this stage in your life? Which seems to be the least developed characteristic? What would you like to achieve in this undeveloped area? Try to be as specific as possible.

E. SUMMARY EXERCISE

What are some of the important things you have learned about yourself after doing these exercises on Allport's trait theory of personality? Which was the most valuable exercise for you? Why?

Classroom Exercise

Join a small discussion group and share with one another what you learned and found important in this unit. After 20 to 30 minutes come together as a whole class and discuss your major learnings.

Abraham Maslow and Self-Actualization Theory

A. Deficiency and Growth Motives
B. Safety Versus Growth
C. Self-Actualization
D. D-love and B-love
E. Peak Experiences
F. Summary Exercise

In 1950, with his publication *Self-Actualizing People: A Study of Psychological Health*, Abraham Maslow laid the foundation for the "third force" humanistic movement in psychology that was to follow some 10 years later.

Maslow was the first psychologist to suggest that the striving for self-actualization was an inherent feature in the structure and process of human motivation. Thus, he was also the first theorist to take a serious interest in the nature and characteristics of the psychologically healthy individual.

Abraham Maslow's creative research and prolific writing, along with his willingness to challenge existing theories and systems, provided much of the inspiration and impetus for the contemporary humanistic revolution in psychology with its emphasis on freeing psychology from the rigidities of psychoanalysis and behaviorism. The name of Abraham Maslow has, therefore, become synonymous with a broader, more humanistically oriented psychology. The development of a more human science has now made topics such as creativity, love and play, spontaneity, personal growth, and higher levels of consciousness respectable areas for serious psychological inquiry. Maslow explored and expanded all of these areas in the course of his career.

In 1969, at the peak of his career and influence, Maslow took a leave of absence from Brandeis University to accept a four-year research grant from the W. P. Laughlin Foundation in Menlo Park, California. During the period of this grant, Dr. Maslow intended to develop a philosophy of democratic politics, economics, and ethics. After a year of work under this grant, Dr. Maslow died of a heart attack on June 8, 1970.

In this unit you will explore some of the creative ideas and theoretical innovations in personality theory that Abraham Maslow brought to us.

A. DEFICIENCY AND GROWTH MOTIVES

One of the most important contributions of Abraham Maslow was his theory of the hierarchy of human motivation. In this theory, Maslow distinguished between two general categories of human motives: *the deficit motives* (deficiency needs) and *growth motives* (metaneeds). The deficit motives are primarily aimed at preventing deprivation of important need areas — *physiological, safety and security, love,* and *self-esteem.*

The growth motives, freed from domination by the deficiency needs, are directed toward self-actualization, toward developing one's potential for achieving wholeness and fulfilling one's highest nature. It will be helpful to distinguish these two primary motivational forces at work in your life.

Exercise 1

a. Make a list of recent actions, motives, and behaviors that reflect deficiency motivation in your life. Try to include an example from each of the deficiency need areas: physiological, safety and security, love, and self-esteem.

b. Make a list of your recent motives and behaviors that are primarily growth motivated — activities and actions that have little or no function in satisfying the deficiency needs but, rather, are concerned with fulfilling your potentials and enhancing your personality development. Think of two or three recent examples of your growth-motivated activities.

c. Appraise the current balance in your life between your deficiency needs and motives and the growth needs and motives. Consider time, energy, money, and other resources devoted to each area.

B. SAFETY VERSUS GROWTH

According to Maslow, one of the basic conflicts throughout life is the conflict we encounter in choosing between safety and growth. Maslow diagramed this conflict thus:

Safety $< - - -$ Person $- - - >$ Growth

One set of forces inhibits us, pulls us back. In the interests of security, we often live our lives clinging to safety and defensiveness, hanging onto the past.

The other set of forces, like a strong wind at our back, urges us forward, invites us to take risks, and impels us toward the self-confident development of our potentials.

This conflict between the growth forces and the defensive and regressive forces within us represents a very basic human dilemma.

Exercise 2

a. Maslow observed that we often have a fear of growth and shy away from developing our best selves (talents, potentials, our own "greatness"). Maslow called this fear of pursuing our highest possibilities the "Jonah complex." Are there specific examples of the Jonah complex in your life? Why do you think we tend to be ambivalent about developing our highest possibilities? Discuss.

b. Identify one or two important decisions or choices you have made in the last few years that represent a yielding to the requirements of safety and security. Keep in mind that we do not necessarily *experience* making a *choice* in many of these decisions and directions taken.

c. Identify one or two important decisions or choices you have made in the last few years that were primarily in the interests of growth and self-actualization.

d. Reflect on the significance and power of each set of motivational forces (safety versus growth) in your life. Are you aware of the tension and struggle between them when you make important decisions? In which direction do you tend to move when faced with such a conflict? Discuss and give examples from recent experience.

C. SELF-ACTUALIZATION

The concept of *self-actualization* is an important one in humanistic psychology and forms the very core of Maslow's theory of motivation and personality development. For Maslow, self-actualized living is the ultimate achievement in the development of the human personality.

In a unique study involving historical figures, prominent people, friends, and college students, Maslow developed a composite picture of the healthy personality or the self-actualizing individual. From this study Maslow outlined 15 identifying characteristics of the self-actualizing person. Some of these characteristics may be applicable to you in your present stage of personality development.

Many of us are still in the process of satisfying deficiency needs, and the purpose of this exercise is not to magnify your weaknesses. It is, rather, to present you with another model of health and maturity, one ideal against which you can appraise your own development and progress within the life process directed toward self-actualization.

Following is a list of Maslow's fifteen characteristics of the self-actualizing individual. Familiarize yourself with the distinctive features of each characteristic. A description of each is found in a number of textbooks on personality theory.

PERSONALITY CHARACTERISTICS
OF THE SELF-ACTUALIZING INDIVIDUAL

1. Efficient perception of reality
2. Acceptance of self, others, and nature
3. Spontaneity, simplicity, and naturalness
4. Problem centering
5. Detachment: need for privacy
6. Autonomy
7. Continued freshness of appreciation
8. Peak or mystic experience
9. Social interest
10. Interpersonal relations
11. Democratic character structure
12. Discrimination between means and ends
13. Sense of philosophical humor
14. Creativeness
15. Resistance to enculturation

Exercise 3

Identify and illustrate three characteristics of the self-actualizing individual that you feel are the *most well developed* in your own personality. Then identify three that you feel are the *most undeveloped* at the present time. (Number each characteristic.)

The three characteristics most fully developed in my personality are:

The three characteristics most undeveloped in my personality are:

Exercise 4

In your experience, what person comes the closest to representing the self-actualizing personality? Briefly describe this person's outstanding features that parallel some of Maslow's characteristics.

D. D-LOVE AND B-LOVE

In his work *Toward a Psychology of Being* (1968), Maslow differentiated between two types of love, which he referred to as *D-love* (or deficiency-love, love that develops out of a sense of deficiency, "love hunger," selfish love) and *B-love* (or being-love, love that is growth motivated, love for the *being* of the other, "unneeding love," unselfish love).

The marked contrasts represented in Maslow's D- and B-love types provide an excellent example of the qualitative superiority inherent in self-actualizing relationships.

After you have completed the following exercises, turn to Appendix A to compare Maslow's distinctions between D- and B-love with your own experiences.

Exercise 5

a. Write a profile of the unhealthiest, most negative love relationship you have ever experienced. Discuss the unhealthy characteristics in this relationship as you experienced them.

b. What impact did this negative relationship have on you?

Exercise 6

a. Write a profile of the healthiest, most rewarding love relationship you have ever experienced. What were the major characteristics of this relationship?

b. Maslow stated that B-love experiences help "create the partner." In what way or ways are you a different person now after experiencing your healthy love relationship? What did you learn and how have you changed? What difference has it made in your personality?

E. PEAK EXPERIENCES

Maslow discovered that self-actualizing individuals frequently enjoy what he termed *peak experiences*. These experiences are the ecstatic moments in life, moments of rapture and intensity. The peak experience is a natural "turn-on" without the aid of drugs.

The phenomenon of the peak experience became a major interest of Maslow's during the latter portion of his career. He believed that the peak experience was a pure moment of self-actualization and an acute identity experience for the individual.

Maslow studied the peak experience in the lives of many individuals. Much of his information regarding the nature and value of the peak experience came from a study of 80 personal interviews and from written responses by 190 college students. In obtaining these written responses, Maslow (1968) presented the student group with the following instructions:

> I would like you to think of the most wonderful experience or experiences of your life; happiest moments, ecstatic moments, moments of rapture, perhaps from being in love, or from listening to music or suddenly "being hit" by a book or a painting, or from some great creative moment. First, list these. And then try to tell me how you feel in such acute moments, how you feel differently from the way you feel at other times, how you are at the moment a different person in some ways. (p. 71)

Exercise 7

a. Respond to Maslow's instructions above as if you were participating in his study.

b. Comment on the significance of your peak experience in altering your perceptions of yourself and the world and in contributing to your personal identity and development.

F. SUMMARY EXERCISE

What are some of the important things you have learned about yourself after doing these exercises on Maslow's theory of personality? Which was the most valuable exercise for you? Why?

Classroom Exercise

Join a small discussion group and share with one another what you learned and found important in this unit. After 20 to 30 minutes come together as a whole class and discuss your major learnings.

Carl Rogers
and
Self-Theory

A. Congruence, Empathic Understanding, and Unconditional Positive Regard
B. The Therapeutic Relationship
C. Conditions of Worth
D. Trusting Your Own Experience
E. Active Listening and Empathic Understanding
F. Summary Exercise

Dr. Carl Rogers was one of the most important and esteemed psychologists of our time. He served as president of the American Psychological Association and is the only psychologist to be awarded both of the major awards of that Association. In 1956 Dr. Rogers was awarded the Distinguished Scientific Contribution Award for his pioneering research on psychotherapy. It was through this early research that Rogers discovered the three therapeutic conditions essential for client change and growth: *congruence, empathic understanding*, and *unconditional positive regard*. In this unit we will explore these and related concepts that are essential components of Rogers' self-theory.

As you are studying Rogers and exploring yourself from the Rogerian perspective it is important to keep in mind that the most central concept in Rogers' self-theory is the *actualizing tendency*.

Every facet of Rogers' (1963) theory is related to and revolves around this master motive " . . . toward actualizing, toward maintenance and enhancement of the organism" (p. 6). The actualizing tendency, as a dynamic life force, becomes the integrating center for all of our experiences, and Rogers' theory of personality development and his approach to psychotherapy cannot be appreciated without understanding the significance of this sovereign motive.

A. CONGRUENCE, EMPATHIC UNDERSTANDING, AND UNCONDITIONAL POSITIVE REGARD

No one since Freud has had a greater impact on the theory and practice of psychotherapy than Carl Rogers. Early in his career he presented the radical claim, supported by his pioneering research, that there were only three therapeutic conditions necessary and sufficient for client change and growth. These are *congruence* (to be real, "open and honest" in the relationship); *empathic understanding* (to understand the feelings and thoughts of the other and to communicate this understanding in the relationship); and *unconditional positive regard* (to accept the other person unconditionally, without evaluating or judging, to like and prize the other).

Rogers believed that these three conditions necessary for therapeutic change are also the environmental conditions necessary to ensure healthy personality development. These environmental conditions nurture the child's healthy growth as sunlight, water, and proper temperature nurture healthy plant life.

Exercise 1

As you understand the meaning and significance of these three conditions for growth, are you aware of their presence or absence in your life? In terms of their relative presence or absence, can you identify the impact of these three conditions on your present development?

B. THE THERAPEUTIC RELATIONSHIP

Rogers hypothesizes that the professional relationship established by the therapist is only a special instance of a lawfulness governing *all* relationships. That is, *any* relationship will be therapeutic and become growth enhancing if it provides the three nurturing conditions for growth.

Your own experience may provide even more meaning and significance to Rogers' hypothesis. With this in mind, respond to the following exercise.

Exercise 2

a. Think of the deepest, most meaningful relationship you have ever experienced with another person (that is, a unique interpersonal relationship that has brought out or enhanced your best qualities and that has promoted your growth and maturity as an individual, a relationship that has contributed significantly to a feeling of well-being). (Rule out parents and other family members in this exercise.) What was the nature of the relationship? Paint a word picture of it as best you can.

b. What did your friend contribute to the relationship?

   c. What did you contribute to the relationship?

   d. Try to identify the influence that this therapeutic relationship has had upon your life and personality and the changes that have come about as a result. Then turn to Appendix B and compare these changes with Rogers' research on the directions that clients take in client-centered psychotherapy.

C. CONDITIONS OF WORTH

The imposition of conditions of worth upon the child leads to a denial or distortion of important self-experiences in order to meet the innate need for positive regard from parents. Certain experiences are, therefore, valued and incorporated into the self-structure only if they are perceived as meeting parental approval. The child may thus disregard the validity of his or her own experiences and organismic evaluations. The child's response to conditions of worth often results, therefore, in a divided self, which Rogers refers to as a state of incongruence. This suggests two central concepts in Rogerian theory:

1. Our innate need for *positive regard*
2. The self-compromises we each make as children to meet certain *conditions of worth* that our parents imposed upon us

In other words, we learn to play roles, deceive our own nature, and follow our parents' script in order to receive attention, approval, and positive regard.

Sheldon Kopp (1977), a psychotherapist and author, provides us with an insightful statement of these Rogerian principles. Kopp has observed that

too often, as children, we are encouraged to try to be something other than ourselves. It is demanded that we assume a character not our own, live out a life-story written by another. The plot line is given. Improvisations are unacceptable, and the direction is an oppressive form of close-quarter tyranny. Neurosis is in part the result of being miscast into a scenario plotted out in accord with somebody else's unfulfilled dreams and unfaced anxieties. (p. 4)

Exercise 3

a. To continue with Sheldon Kopp's metaphor, do you feel at times that you have been miscast and are following someone else's script? Discuss.

b. It must be emphasized that very few of us have experienced *unconditional* positive regard. Thus, we are likely to manifest both congruence and incongruence in our development. Combining Rogers' concepts of congruence and incongruence with Kopp's metaphor, sketch both aspects of your personality in the following exercise.

- *Your incongruent self* (meeting conditions of worth in order to win approval and positive regard). Describe the *character* you play, unwittingly perhaps, when you are "on stage."

- *Your congruent (real) self*. Describe the person you feel you genuinely are.

Exercise 4

Select a current issue or problem in your life where there is a conflict between your stage character (incongruent self) and your more congruent, genuine self. Write a dialogue between your incongruent self and your real self. What would your real self like to say to your stage character? Let this be a spontaneous interaction between these two conflicting aspects of your personality.

REAL SELF:

STAGE CHARACTER:

REAL SELF:

STAGE CHARACTER:

REAL SELF:

STAGE CHARACTER:

REAL SELF:

STAGE CHARACTER:

REAL SELF:

D. TRUSTING YOUR OWN EXPERIENCE

Carl Rogers believes that the inability to make decisions or to choose wisely comes as a result of sacrificing the inherent wisdom contained in our own experiences for the wishes and opinions of others in order to receive positive regard. Trusting one's own experience is an important characteristic of Rogers' *fully functioning person* and represents a state of congruence.

Trusting in your own experience is, therefore, an important Rogerian concept and is an important expression of the organismic valuing process. Infants and young children tend to rely on this valuing process easily and naturally.

Exercise 5

a. What important things have you learned (about yourself, "life," the world, etc.) that have come directly from your own experience? What do you know to be true that has come directly from your own experiencing? If possible, indicate the experiences that led to this important personal knowledge.

b. What important choice or decision have you made recently that reflects the validity of your own experience and the organismic valuing process at work?

E. ACTIVE LISTENING AND EMPATHIC UNDERSTANDING

In a statement on the profound value of empathy in psychotherapy and in healthy interpersonal relationships, Rogers states that "over the years . . . the research evidence has kept piling up, and it points strongly to the conclusion that a high degree of empathy in a relationship is possibly the most potent factor in bringing about change and learning" (1980, p. 139).

An empathic person must know how to listen. An active, empathic listener responds to feelings and to "felt" meanings in the communication, will enter the private world of meanings and feelings of the other and see them as he or she does, and will enter this private world and respond to it without moral judgments or evaluations.

Classroom Exercise

a. Get a partner and find a little private space in which to talk. (If it is not feasible to do this as a classroom activity, arrange to do these exercises with a partner outside class.) Designate who will be student A and student B.

• Student A is to talk for three minutes while student B actively listens. Student A may talk about anything of current interest to himself or herself. Following the 3-minute period, student B will repeat back to student A as much of the cognitive content as possible in a way that is as true to student A's message as possible. Student A should remind student B of any omissions and correct any distortions that appear in the restatement of the communication.

• Now switch roles. Student A becomes the active listener and student B is to talk for three minutes.

b. Again, divide into pairs and find your private space.

• This time student A is to talk for three minutes on something that is *emotionally significant* in his or her life *at the present time.* (Do not violate your own sense of privacy, but talk of a current difficulty or pleasure in your life that you feel comfortable in sharing.) Student B is to listen, this time, for emotional or affective (feeling) messages. When student A completes the three-minute communication, student B is to respond with empathic understanding, stressing those *feelings* he or she heard being expressed. Student A again confirms or corrects student B's responses. Discuss this interaction after you have finished.

• Switch roles and follow the same directions.

Exercise 6

a. Respond with empathic understanding to the following statements.[1] Think of yourself as a counselor in responding to these communications. After reading each client's presentation, write your response *exactly* as you would respond to the person. Remember, you are to respond with empathic understanding, so try not to diagnose, ask questions, judge, evaluate, or give advice. Try to keep your responses short and uncomplicated. After you have completed your responses, check Appendix C for some examples of good and poor responses to each client's statement.

---

[1]Statements in this Exercise section are reprinted by permission from S. Wolf, C. M. Wolf, & G. Spielberg, *The Wolf Counseling Skills Evaluation Handbook* (Omaha: National Publication, 1980), pp. 43, 47–48.

• *First client.* "I don't know what to do about my son. He is 16 now. I can't talk to him — can't reach him. It's like he's in another world. He resents our affluence, the way we dress, our friends, the way we think. You know, when I look at him, eye to eye, my own son, I see hatred."

Response:

• *Second client.* "It's really hard to talk to you — but that's my problem. They say I'm shy, but it's worse than that. I want to hide when people are around. I can't look at them."

Response:

• *Third client.* "This probation officer said I had to come here. He said I did a really 'bad' thing. Yeah, I got busted for smoking grass. I'm a real criminal! You can get smashed on your cocktails, but if we're caught smoking pot, then we get nailed. So what are you going to do now, cure the 'bad' marijuana addict?"

Response:

b. Respond with empathic understanding to the following messages. This time, think of yourself as a friend in responding to these communications. Write your *verbatim responses* exactly as you would respond to your friend. Remember, make *empathic* responses.

• *Woman, age 18.* "I tell you, I hate my father. And there's no reason for it. He is a minister—a good and righteous man. He has never laid a hand on me. But I have this terrific feeling against him, and it makes me feel so terrible . . . because there is no reason for it."

Response:

• *Man, age 21.* "Shall I marry her? Or shall I think of my future? If a fellow is going to think of his future—if he's got ambition and drive to get ahead—he's got to be hard and forget all about sentiment. But I do love Marie—I really do. If we broke off, I don't know what I'd do."

Response:

Classroom Exercise

After you have completed the exercise above, divide into small groups of four to six or slightly larger, if necessary, and discuss your responses to both of the verbal messages. First, try to identify the feelings each person is expressing or trying to express. Then share your own responses and discuss each in terms of the degree of empathy expressed.

F. SUMMARY EXERCISE

What are some of the important things you have learned about yourself after doing these exercises on Rogers' self-theory of personality? Which was the most valuable exercise for you? Why?

Classroom Exercise

Join a small discussion group and share with one another what you learned and found important in this unit. After 20 to 30 minutes come together as a whole class and discuss your major learnings.

APPENDICES
REFERENCES
ABOUT THE AUTHOR

APPENDIX A

Maslow's D-Love and B-Love

The following characteristics of D-Love and B-Love are presented by Maslow in his *Toward a Psychology of Being* (1968, pp. 42-43). After you complete Exercises 5 and 6 in Section D of Unit Nine, compare your responses with these characteristics.

D-Love

D-lovers are dependent on each other in unhealthy ways.

D-lovers are in frequent conflict. There is a high degree of anxiety–hostility in the relationship.

D-lovers do not change, grow, and mature in the relationship.

D-love is possessive and restricting.

B-Love

B-love has a widespread therapeutic effect. Partners change and grow in the experience.

B-lovers are more independent of each other, less jealous.

B-lovers have a minimum of anxiety–hostility toward each other.

B-love is nonpossessive.

B-love is always pleasure-giving and intrinsically enjoyable.

Rogers and Client-Centered Psychotherapy

The following directions taken by clients in client-centered psychotherapy are adapted from Rogers' *On Becoming a Person* (1961, pp. 167-175). After you complete Exercise 2 in Section B of Unit Ten, compare your response with these directions.

Away from facades — moving away from a self that he or she is *not*

Away from "oughts" — moving from a compelling image of what he or she "ought to be"

Away from meeting expectations — moving away from what the culture expects him or her to be

Away from pleasing others — moving away from being defined by the needs of others

Toward self-direction — becoming more independent and more autonomous

Toward openness to experience — becoming freer to experience the self

Toward greater acceptance of others

Toward greater trust of self

Rogers and Empathic Understanding

Rogers believes that active listening and empathic understanding are very important in bringing about change and learning. In Exercise 6, Section E, of Unit Ten, you were to respond with empathic understanding to three statements. Compare your responses with the following responses, which are rated by judges on a five-point rating scale.[1] In each case, is your response closer to Response A or Response B?

Statement #1

Response A: "Wow, that must feel overpowering; to think that someone you love and have brought up might hate you and what you stand for."

Judges' comments: "This response is potent, empathic, and sums up the essence of the statement succinctly and graphically. Rating: 5.0."

Response B: "Are you trying to force your values down his throat? Can you let him begin to develop his own sense of what is right for him? Give him the choice of choosing how he wants to live. Let go of him!"

Judges' comments: "This judgmental and angry statement is a projection of the counselor's own views. It is advice-giving, directive, and intolerant. Rating: 1.0."

Statement #2

Response A: "Any contact with people is so threatening and frightening that you wish you could disappear — and it's getting worse and worse."

Judges' comments: "This powerfully empathic statement communicates the essence of the client's message and much more. It is a superlative counselor response. Rating: 5.0."

Response B: "Do you really want to be outgoing, or is it easier to hide?"

Judges' comments: "This statement would probably shock the client. It is a strong confrontation, disrespectful, and will probably push the client further into her shell. Rating: 1.0."

Statement #3

Response A: "You feel you've been unfairly treated, and that my vices are as bad as yours — maybe worse."

Judges' comments: "Immediate, potent, and empathic, this statement indicates the counselor is unafraid to say exactly what has been perceived. It makes the situa-

---

[1]These responses and judges' comments are reprinted by permission from S. Wolf, C. M. Wolf, & G. Spielberg, *The Wolf Counseling Skills Evaluation Handbook* (Omaha: National Publication, 1980), pp. 43, 47-48.

tion personal and is accurately, concisely, and non-defensively reflected. Rating: 4.5."

Response B: "Let's hold off for a minute, eh? I have to get some information, then we'll talk."

Judges' comments: "This statement indicates the counselor is attempting to control the situation and is sarcastic and disrespectful in manner. It communicates that the 'information' is more important than the client's present feelings. Rating: 1.0."

References

Erikson, E. (1959). *Identity and the life cycle: Selected papers.* New York: International Universities Press.

Erikson, E. (1964). *Insight and responsibility.* New York: W. W. Norton.

Hjelle, L., & Ziegler, D. J. (1981). *Personality theories: Basic assumptions, research, and applications,* 2nd ed. New York: McGraw-Hill.

Horney, K. (1937). *The neurotic personality of our time.* New York: W. W. Norton.

Horney, K. (1966). *Our inner conflicts.* New York: W. W. Norton.

Horney, K. (1970). *Neurosis and human growth.* New York: W. W. Norton.

Kopp, S. (1977). *This side of tragedy.* Palo Alto, CA: Science and Behavior Books.

Maslow, A. (1950). Self-actualizing people: A study of psychological health. In W. Wolff (Ed.), *Values in personality research* (pp. 11-34). New York: Grune and Stratton.

Maslow, A. (1968). *Toward a psychology of being,* 2nd ed. New York: D. Van Nostrand.

Rogers, C. R. (1961). *On becoming a person.* Boston: Houghton Mifflin.

Rogers, C. R. (1963). The actualizing tendency. In M. R. Jones (Ed.), *Nebraska symposium on motivation,* Vol. 11. Lincoln: University of Nebraska Press.

Rogers, C. R. (1980). *A way of being.* Boston: Houghton Mifflin.

Williams, R. L., & Long, J. D. (1979). *Toward a self-managed life style,* 2nd ed. Boston: Houghton Mifflin.

Wolf, S., Wolf, C. M., & Spielberg, G. (1980). *The Wolf counseling skills evaluation handbook.* Omaha: National Publication.

About the Author

Willard Frick is Professor of Psychology at Albion College where he teaches courses in personality theory and humanistic psychology. He is the author of numerous publications in the areas of personality theory and psychotherapy. A practicing psychotherapist, Dr. Frick is currently on the staff of Oaklawn Psychological Services, Marshall, Michigan. He is a member of the Association for Humanistic Psychology and serves as an Associate Editor of the *Journal of Humanistic Psychology*.